Local Government in North Carolina

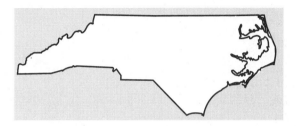

Gordon P. Whitaker
The University of North Carolina at Chapel Hill

North Carolina City and County
Management Association
Raleigh, NC

ABOUT THE AUTHOR

Gordon P. Whitaker received his Ph.D. from Indiana University. He began teaching at the University of North Carolina in Chapel Hill in 1973. Dr. Whitaker directs the Master of Public Administration (MPA) Program at The University of North Carolina at Chapel Hill and is proud to call Durham, NC home. He takes great pride in his work preparing students for careers in public service. He has generously volunteered his experience and time writing this book for the students and citizens of North Carolina.

Cover Art and Design: Randall Goodall/ Seventeenth Street Studios
Interior Design and Production: Nikki Navta/ Navta Associates, Inc.
Cartoons: Stephen Rustad/ Stephen Rustad and Associates
Project Management: Catherine Rossbach/ BMR

 This book is printed on 60# Troy Book Opaque Smooth stock. It is composed of 50% recycled fiber and 10% post consumer waste.

North Carolina City and County Management Association
215 North Dawson Street, Raleigh, NC 27602

ISBN 0-938545-07-8

Library of Congress Catalog Card Number : 93-084513

Printed in the United States of America.

First Printing

Contents

Photo Credits

p. 1—Gary D. Knight, CCBI, Wake County, NC

p. 2—*The Wilson Daily Times*

p. 3—Dixie B. O'Conner, *Southern City*, North Carolina League of Municipalities

p. 4—Bruce Egan, Department of City and Regional Planning, UNC/Chapel Hill

p. 7—City of Fayetteville, NC

p. 10—Eric J. Peterson, Town Manager, Town of Topsail Beach, NC

p. 11—Dorothy Brown Smith, Public Service and Information Officer, City of Rocky Mount, NC

p. 13—Ole Gade, Boone, NC

p. 15—North Carolina Collection, Pack Memorial Public Library, Asheville, NC

p. 16—North Carolina Division of Archives and History

p. 17—North Carolina Collection, University of North Carolina at Chapel Hill

p. 21—Dorothy Brown Smith, Public Service and Information Officer, City of Rocky Mount, NC

p. 24—Brenda T. Patterson, *The Franklin Times*

p. 25—Marguerite B. McCall

p. 26—Gary D. Knight, CCBI, Wake County, NC

p. 27—North Carolina Division of Archives and History

p. 28–29—Reprinted, by permission of the publisher, from *North Carolina, The History of a Southern State,* by Hugh Talmage Lefler and Albert Ray Newsome. Copyright ©1954 by the University of North Carolina Press.

p. 31—Bruce Egan, Department of City and Regional Planning, UNC/Chapel Hill

p. 32—Ole Gade, Boone, NC

p. 36—Richard Y. Stevens, Wake County Manager

p. 39—Gary D. Knight, CCBI, Wake County, NC

p. 41—Gayle Butzgy, *County Lines,* North Carolina Association of County Commissioners

p. 43—Mike Decker, *The Franklin Press*

p. 45—Gary D. Knight, CCBI, Wake County, NC

p. 48—Alisha Ashe, *The Franklin Press*

p. 49—Alisha Ashe, *The Franklin Press*

p. 51—City of Fayetteville

p. 53—David R. Allen, *The Liberty News*

p. 55—*Asheville Citizen-Times*

p. 57—City of Fayetteville, NC

p. 59—*Fayetteville Observer-Times*

p. 61—Pete Lannon

p. 62—City of Winston-Salem Public Information Office

p. 65—City of Fayetteville, NC

p. 66—Aaron P. Noble, Jr., Director of Public Information, City of Burlington, NC

p. 67—City of Winston-Salem Public Information Office

p. 70—City of Fayetteville, NC

p. 71—Bill Stice, Town of Cary, NC

p. 74—*Fayetteville Observer-Times*

p. 79—City of Fayetteville, NC

p. 84—Dorothy Brown Smith, Public Service and Information Officer, City of Rocky Mount, NC

p. 89—Don Hunter

p. 90—Ole Gade, Boone, NC

p. 91—City of Fayetteville, NC

p. 95—City of Raleigh, NC

p. 97—*The Herald-Sun*, Durham, NC

p. 105—City of Winston-Salem Public Information Office

p. 106—Dorothy Brown-Smith, Public Service and Information Officer, City of Rocky Mount, NC

p. 107—City of Fayetteville, NC

p. 108—Alice B. Freeman

p. 114—City of Fayetteville, NC

p. 116—Dorothy Brown Smith, Public Service and Information Officer, City of Rocky Mount, NC

p. 118—Vernon Malone, Chairman, Wake County Board of Commissioners

p. 120—Dorothy Brown Smith, Public Service and Information Officer, City of Rocky Mount, NC

p. 122—Bill Nash, Public Affairs Officer, Guilford County, NC

p. 126—Asher Johnson, Associate Editor, *The Franklin Times*

Preface

Local government—the level of government closest to the people—is often taken for granted. Yet take away the services provided by local governments in North Carolina, everything from schools to running water to law enforcement, and modern life would be nearly impossible. Counties and municipalities deliver the essential services day in, day out. And North Carolina local governments enjoy a well-deserved reputation for excellence and integrity.

Delivering critical services efficiently is no easy task, and many local officials feel that governing is becoming even more difficult. They also believe that informed and involved citizens are necessary for a well-run local government.

Every ninth grader in North Carolina public schools studies economics, law, and politics, but few textbooks previously used in such courses offered much information on local governments. And, certainly, almost none provide information on Tar Heel cities, towns, and counties.

Recognizing the importance of educating students about their local governments, the North Carolina City and County Management Association began this book project. The association's goals were to raise the level of awareness about the state's local governments and how they are run, to show how local governments affect everyday life, and to interest students in participating in local government.

Producing this book mirrors much of what is good about local government in North Carolina—people working together to achieve a common goal. *Local Government in North Carolina* is a joint effort made possible by the dedicated work of many people, as well as funding from several organizations and hundreds of counties and municipalities.

Early on, the managers' association asked the North Carolina League of Municipalities and the North Carolina Association of County Commissioners to join in the effort. Both did so by giving funds directly and by leading the fund-raising efforts. The North Carolina Department of Public Instruction and the Institute of Government at the University of North Carolina at Chapel Hill also are supporters of this project.

Dr. Gordon P. Whitaker, a professor of political science and director of the master's program in public administration at UNC-Chapel Hill, is the author of this book. The North Carolina City and County Management Association owes its deepest gratitude to Dr. Whitaker for his efforts. Dr. Whitaker donated his knowledge, his talents, and his time to this project. His book will help tens of thousands of North Carolinians know more about their local governments.

Hundreds of individual counties and municipalities also played a major role in this book. These local governments voluntarily contributed a fee, based on their population, to pay for printing this book. The Association extends its thanks for this tremendous support. A listing of the cities, towns, and counties that contributed funds appears at the end of the book.

Giving this book to ninth-grade students is one step in the Association's educational efforts. We expect to work with individual schools and their teachers to make local government come alive for students. We hope to bring local officials into the classroom and to involve students in their local governments. We hope that, through these efforts, the next generation will be both informed and interested in their local governments.

Carolyn H. Carter

Carolyn H. Carter
President, 1992–1993
North Carolina City and County Management Association

Acknowledgements

Many people have helped me write this book. Their contributions have made it more accurate, more interesting, and easier to read. Their good-humored help also made my work on the book a real pleasure. I thank them all.

My thanks first go to my research assistants on this project: Hana Kohn, Tim Leshan, Marcy Onieal, Eric C. Peterson, and Roger Schlegel. They located materials and provided many useful ideas and suggestions on various versions of the manuscript.

The MPA office staff, Jean Coble and Kathy Frymoyer, helped me coordinate the project with the North Carolina City and County Management Association (NCCCMA). I thank them for attending so well to all the details of project administration.

I also thank my faculty colleagues for their careful review of the manuscript. Dr. Carolyn Grubbs of Meredith College, Dr. Nanette Mengel of the University of North Carolina at Chapel Hill MPA Program, and Professors David Lawrence and Warren J. Wicker of the UNC Institute of Government each gave me valuable suggestions in response to drafts of the book.

Several high-school teachers also took time to read earlier versions of the book. Their comments and suggestions were particularly helpful, as I sought to write this book for them and their students. I appreciate greatly the help of James T. Coble, Hickory High School, Hickory; Judy Daniels, Hoggard High School, Wilmington; Pat Gurley, Mt. Olive Junior High School, Mt. Olive; Ann Heafner, West Lincoln High School, Lincolnton; Vennie James, Smithfield-Selma High School, Smithfield; Ricky McDevitt, Madison High School, Marshall; Marcie Pachino, Jordan High School, Durham; Peggy Shonosky, Laney High School, Wilmington; and Darnell Tabron, Jordan High School, Durham. Doug Robertson and John Ellington of the NC State Department of Public Instruction provided valuable assistance.

Catherine Rossbach of BMR coordinated publication of the book with apparent ease and obvious good will. She made the task of turning a manuscript into a book smooth and pleasant. I thank her most warmly for her help. I also thank Ursula Szwast for her many good editorial suggestions. I only hope I adopted enough of them.

Local government leaders have also helped make this book possible. Through the NCCCMA, North Carolina city and county managers are the publishers of this book. The members of the NCCCMA Civic Education Committee and Reading Committee provided valuable direction for this project. City council members and county commissioners all across the state voted to pay to make this book available to the state's public-school students. The names of the participating counties and municipalities are listed at the end of the book. Many local government professionals also shared with me their comments and suggestions on drafts of the manuscript. My special thanks go to Raymond Boutwell, Wake County; Margot Christensen, NC League of Municipalities; Scott Dadson, Fairmont; Terry Henderson, NC League of Municipalities; Debra Henzey, NC Association of County Commissioners; James Hipp, Lenoir; J. Thomas Lundy, Catawba County; R. Lee Matthews, Hamlet; J. Michael Moore, Thomasville; Robert Shepherd, Land-of-Sky Regional Council; Robert Shepherd, Jr., Kernersville; Kenneth Windley, Davie County; and John Witherspoon, Cabarrus County.

Most especially, I want to thank Carolyn Carter, NCCCMA President, and Bob Slade, Chair of the NCCCMA Civic Education Committee, for their encouragement and support. They provided the leadership that directed and sustained this project.

Gordon P. Whitaker

Gordon P. Whitaker
Chapel Hill

Local Government and You

Local governments affect our lives in many ways. They supply the water we drink. They provide police and fire protection. They operate the public schools, parks, and libraries. They help people in need. They regulate how land is used and enforce state and local laws. They work to bring new jobs to their communities. Local governments are important to you because they help determine how well you and your neighbors live.

This book is about local governments (cities, towns, and counties) in North Carolina. This book explores the ways that local government affects people and the ways that people can influence their local government. This book examines the ways local governments are organized and the ways they operate. This book also focuses on the people who make local government work.

PURPOSES OF LOCAL GOVERNMENT

The purpose of local government is to make life better for the people in the community. Local governments try to do this in three ways:

1. Local governments provide services. Water supply, fire protection, schools, parks, and libraries are among the many services they provide. Some services are used by everyone every day. Other services help people with special needs or help people in times of crisis.

2. Local governments encourage community improvement. The ways they do this include encouraging new businesses, sponsoring community festivals and clean-up days, and organizing human-relations commissions.

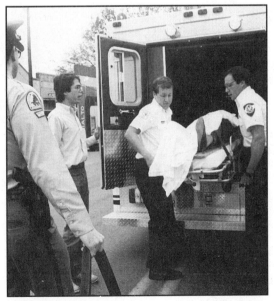

Serving people.

3. Local governments protect people against harmful behavior. Making and enforcing laws to protect the public are important local government responsibilities. Although the state government in North Carolina makes most of the criminal laws, local law enforcement agencies investigate most of the crimes and make most of the arrests. Crime is not the only kind of harmful behavior, of course. People can also harm others without meaning to do so. Local governments set regulations to prevent this. For example, local governments might restrict factories from locating next to houses, or they might regulate where people park their cars.

Improving the community.

Responding to Disaster

The winds from Hurricane Hugo struck Mecklenburg County, North Carolina, a couple of hours after midnight. The storm tore trees from the ground, sending them through roofs and across power lines and streets. By the time the sun rose on September 22, 1989, the entire Charlotte area was paralyzed by storm damage.

- Most streets and roads were blocked by fallen trees.
- 75% of the houses were without electricity.
- Most telephone service was out.
- 30 of 37 sewer pump stations were out of service. This meant that people were unable to drain the water from their sinks or flush their toilets.
- 438 out of 458 traffic lights were not working.
- Half of all street gutters and drains were blocked, causing extensive flooding.
- More than $370 million worth of damage was done to houses and businesses.

Luckily for the residents of Charlotte and Mecklenburg county, city and county governments were prepared for just such an emergency. They took immediate action to protect public health and safety. The Emergency Management Office is a joint city/county agency responsible for handling disasters such as the damge done by Hugo. The people in that office directed the response and aid to relieve the effects of Hugo's damage.

Clean-up and recovery was a cooperative effort of city and county employees, state workers, electric and phone company employees, and the residents themselves. Altogether, more than 25 city, county, and state agencies were involved in the relief efforts. More than 600 city and county police, state highway patrol officers, and national guard personnel controlled traffic and protected property against looting. Firefighters set up large ponds of fresh water at various places near where people were without running water in their houses. Another 1000 public employees worked night and day to clear the streets and restore public services. Employees of the electric company and the telephone compant also worked long hours, replacing the broken lines. Everywhere, residents themselves worked to help clear highways, streets, and sidewalks, as well as their own homes. Working together, local governments coordinated both the immediate response to the crisis and the rebuilding after the storm.

Protecting people.

The United States; North Carolina; Union County.

NATIONAL, STATE, AND LOCAL GOVERNMENTS

When people speak about "the government" they often mean the United States government, but we have several types of governments in this country. We have a **federal** system of government. National, state, and local governments each have their areas of responsibility and authority. The national government in Washington, D.C., is responsible for dealing with problems that affect the entire country. We often call our national government the "federal government" because it is made up of states. North Carolina is one of fifty states that make up the United States of America. Each state government is responsible for problems within its **jurisdiction**. Each state also has established local governments to deal with the particular "close to home" needs of the people.

Each government has the responsibility to serve the best interests of all its people, the authority to make and enforce laws and to provide services, and the authority to tax to raise funds to support its work.

Each citizen of the United States is also a citizen of the state in which he or she lives. Citizens of North Carolina are also citizens of the county in which they live. People who live within city or town limits are also citizens of that **municipality**. Each level of government—federal, state, county, and municipal—is governed by elected officials. Each level of government provides certain services, regulates certain kinds of activity, and undertakes programs to improve public well-being.

The national government makes laws and carries out policies that affect the entire country. The United States Constitution, for example, applies to all residents of the United States and to all governments in the United States. State and local governments may not pass or enforce laws that contradict the Constitution. For example, the Constitution requires that state and local governments provide "equal protection under the law" to all people.

Among the services operated by the federal government are mail delivery, Social Security benefit payments, and recreation opportunities in national parks, forests, and recreation areas. The national government regulates activities such as the manufacture and sale of medicines, the sale of stocks and bonds, and the operation of nuclear electrical generating plants. National government programs for the general well-being include defense, research, and transportation. The Army, Navy, and Air Force provide national defense. The National Science Foundation, the National Institutes of Health, and other agencies support studies of diseases and possible cures. Federal grants support highway and airport construction.

Federal—
a system with separate state and national governments. The United States has a **federal** system of government. We also use the term "federal government" to refer to the national government of the United States.

Jurisdiction—
the right to use legal authority **or** the territory over which a government can use its authority.

Municipality—
a city, town, or village that has an organized government with authority to make laws, provide services, and collect and spend taxes and other public funds.

The North Carolina state government also provides many services. It is responsible for building, maintaining, and policing the state's highways. State government provides recreation opportunities in state parks, forests, and recreation areas. It helps people locate jobs, and it pays unemployment benefits to those who are unemployed. The state government regulates such matters as insurance rates, waste disposal, and development along the North Carolina coast. Among the state's programs to improve the general well-being are the recruitment of industry to the state, agricultural research, and promotion of the arts.

In the chapters that follow, you will see that federal and state governments influence local governments. One sort of influence involves **mandates** by which federal or state governments require local governments to provide a service or to carry out services in specified ways. Mandates say how counties operate programs of assistance like Medicaid and Food Stamps, for example. Federal and state governments also provide **grants** to help fund some local government programs like police services or housing repairs. Federal and state governments also greatly influence some local governments through their decisions about the location and operation of facilities like hospitals, prisons, parks and forests, and military bases. Closing a hospital or military base, expanding a prison, or changing policies on timber harvest or tourism on state or federal land often has a major impact on the local economy and, therefore, on the local government in whose jurisdiction those facilities are located. In North Carolina, local governments can do

Mandate—
a legal order by which one government requires actions by another government.

Grant—
money given by state or federal government to local governments to fund local projects.

In the News . . .

How Local Government Helps Me

The author of the following essay is Becky Sanderson, an eighth-grade student at Kings Creek School in Caldwell County. As part of National County Government Week, the school system sponsored an essay contest in the middle schools. Miss Sanderson wrote the winning essay.

I lifted my head to the sounds of sirens wailing in the middle of the night. The sirens meant a person being comforted in his or her illness, a life being saved, and people working hard.

The next morning I found out that an elderly woman had suffered a stroke in the middle of the night. Her husband had called the emergency service. The ambulance had come to the rescue.

While I was watching the news, my mom was calling the health department to make an appointment for my sister to have her booster shots.

I finished breakfast. Afterwards I took out the trash for the trash men to pick up.

I hurried to catch the school

bus. While on the bus, I thought about my morning.

If there weren't a local and state government, I would be deprived of many everyday luxuries that I have. Many other people might not be alive because there were no local health departments, hospitals, fire stations, or many other government offices and such.

—adapted from
County Lines, XVII, No. 9
May 22, 1991

only those things the state government gives them authority to do. Thus, the state can also prevent local governments from doing things opposed to state policy.

Local governments focus on local issues. Like other governments, they provide services, make and enforce laws, and collect taxes to support their work. Local governments also have the responsibility to serve and protect everyone in their jurisdiction. Everyone in the local government's jurisdiction is responsible for obeying local laws and paying local taxes. This includes not only the residents of the jurisdiction but also people who work, shop, or visit there and people who own property there. Everyone, regardless of place of residence, has the right to be treated fairly by local government officials of every local jurisdiction in the United States.

Often there is considerable overlap between local issues and broader interests. One town's use of a river to carry away its waste water can interfere with the use of that same river as a water supply by towns downstream. Local governments often work closely together to deal with such problems. Most local governments in North Carolina participate in one of the 18 **regional councils** in the state. Local governments join the regional council in their area. They pay dues to support the work of the regional council and appoint representatives to meet to discuss problems they share and to work out ways to deal with those problems. Local governments also cooperate directly with one another. They usually have **mutual aid agreements** to help each other fight fires or deal with other emergencies. Often a county and the municipalities within it work together in various ways, including building libraries or parks, setting up recycling or economic development programs, planning and controlling land use, and collecting taxes.

Regional council—
an organization of local governments to deal with their mutual problems. There are 18 regional councils covering North Carolina.

Mutual aid agreement—
commitments of local governments to assist each other, such as in dealing with emergencies.

Public issues are discussed at a meeting of the Fayetteville City Council.

Population—
all the people who live
in a place.

You and the other residents make up the **population** of your county, city, or town. Together you make up the community that your local government represents. You are the people who most regularly use the services of your local government. Its laws and its community improvement activities affect you. If you have lived in your community very long at all, you probably also identify yourself with your local government and feel some pride in it and loyalty to it.

Any group of people who share common bonds can be thought of as a community, of course. You may also think of yourself as belonging to other communities—a neighborhood or an ethnic or religious group, for example. However, these informal communities do not have governmental authority or responsibility. They play a very different part in your life than do local governments. Local governments have the authority and the responsibility to regulate what people do and to make people pay to support and protect the community.

It is often difficult to decide how best to meet the needs of all the people in a local government's jurisdiction. People may disagree about whether they need another swimming pool or new

In the News . . .

Reduced Traffic Pleases Carolina Ave. Residents

By Theresa Shea
The Herald-Sun

Beth Silberman is a happy woman these days. She worries less about her 2-year old son's safety.

"It's wonderful," says Ms. Silberman. "He can hold my hand when we cross the street now without me having to pick him up."

Ken Rose, Ms. Silberman's husband, agreed. "I feel my child is going to be a lot safer," he said.

Ms. Silberman and Mr. Rose live on Carolina Avenue—for years a favorite rush-hour shortcut for commuters speeding to Duke's West campus medical center.

But perseverance and initiative have paid off for residents of the street. City transportation officials studied traffic on Carolina Avenue and found it to be five times heavier than on nearby streets of the same size. During rush hour, 300 cars—one every 12 seconds—drove down the road.

About six weeks ago the Carolina Neighborhood Association invited the City Council to breakfast.

Putting coffee on one side of the street and cream on the other, residents made council members cross the busy street—and made their point in the process.

Residents followed up the

breakfast by petitioning the council and testifying before the Public Works Committee.

On Wednesday, the city installed four-way stop signs at the intersection of Carolina and Knox street.

"Traffic was a terrible problem for us," said Farley Ransom, president of the Carolina Neighborhood Association. "It was really destroying the street. It's much quieter and less traveled now. It's already much better."
—adapted from
The Durham Herald-Sun
August 22, 1991

tennis courts, about where to locate a landfill or sewage treatment plant, or about the need for sponsoring a teen center. They may disagree about the need to increase local taxes to pay for public services.

Elected officials have the difficult responsibility of deciding what the needs of the community are and what the government should do. As representatives of the people, they have the authority for deciding the policies and programs of local governments. Elected officials select local government employees (either directly or indirectly) and oversee their work. In later chapters we will explore the specific responsibilities of various elected officials.

Local government employees carry out the work of local government. They make sure that safe drinking water is readily available. They answer calls for police assistance, fight fires, maintain public buildings, and help those who need public assistance. Local government employees include lifeguards at the public swimming pool, the public librarian, and the city or county manager. Public employees are responsible for putting local government policies and programs into practice. You will learn more about their work in later chapters.

All those who live, work, own property, or otherwise have an interest in a community have the right to request public services from the local government and to let local government officials know about their concerns. To make concerns known, you can call city, town, or county offices; talk to local elected officials; write letters to the local newspaper; or attend public meetings.

You can learn about local public issues by reading the newspaper, by talking to friends, and, in more and more communities, by watching public-affairs television. You can expand your knowledge of public issues and programs by reading materials from the library and by discussing the issues with local government officials.

Voters in local government jurisdictions have a great impact on local government decisions. Voters can affect decisions by voting for officials who reflect voters' views and concerns and by voting in local **referendums**. In addition to voting, citizens can affect local government decisions by running for and being elected to public office.

*Referendum—
an election in which citizens vote directly on a public policy question.*

LEARNING ABOUT LOCAL GOVERNMENT

When you need public services, where can you get them? How can local governments help you resolve public disputes? What are your responsibilities as a citizen of local government? How can you participate in making your community a better place to live?

Working for Local Government . . .

an interview with
Eric J. Peterson
Town Manager
Topsail Beach, NC

Topsail Beach Manager Eric Peterson (right) discusses beach erosion with the town's public works director, Frank Ricks.

I work for local government for two reasons: 1) the variety that city management has to offer and 2) the opportunity for public service.

What really attracts me, I think, is the public service. That may sound corny, but it's not. In local government, one person can have a positive impact. I can actually see how my actions affect the community.

My daily duties include overseeing town activities. I consult with department heads (such as the chief of police and the public works director) to keep abreast of their activities and to assist in troubleshooting any potential problems. I spend a good deal of time responding to immediate problems that the council or citizens identify. Part of my job, however, is to look ahead and plan so that we can take action before a situation gets to the problem stage. For instance, as town manager I am Topsail Beach's emergency response manager as well. I am responsible for preparing a plan for how to deal with a hurricane or other disaster and for ordering an evacuation of the town if that is needed.

I also act as one of Topsail Beach's contacts with other governments, although the mayor is the town's official representative. Additionally, I provide information to the mayor and council at town meetings. At these meetings, citizens often have questions for the council or for me. If I don't know the answer, I get the person's phone number and call him or her as soon as I find the answer.

Citizen participation is important. I think it is the manager's responsibility to help encourage participation. The more I know people's ideas and opinions, the better able I am to address their needs and problems.

To those in school I have just one bit of advice—get involved! Now is the time you should be learning how to influence government. Sure, you can't vote yet, but you can do many other things. Tour the town hall, the police station, or even the waste treatment plant. Invite local officials to come speak to your class. Attend town meetings. You might even want to volunteer for an internship after school, helping out in local government for a couple of hours a week. The more you know about local government, the better you'll be able to know how to use it to solve local problems.

Working in local government is never dull; and when you do a good job, you know it benefits the community. You can *see* the results.

—Interviewed by Eric C. Peterson

Basketball at the neighborhood park is just one of the many services local governments provide.

Because local governments affect your life in so many ways and because they should be open to your participation and influence, you need to know about your local government. In the chapters that follow, you will learn how North Carolina's cities, towns, and counties provide public services, how they protect the public from harmful activities, and how they improve the community you live in.

This book includes interviews with some of the people who make local governments work. It also includes excerpts from newspaper articles about local government. The interviews and articles are examples of the kinds of information you can collect about local governments in your own part of the state. Some of the terms used to discuss government may have special meanings or be new to you. The glossary in the back of the book defines these words. Terms listed in the glossary are in bold print the first time they appear in the text, and a short definition is in the margin on the same page. If you encounter a word that is unfamiliar, first check the glossary. If it is not included there, check your dictionary.

At the end of this book is a list of books and magazines for further reading about the topics discussed in this book. Many of these books and magazines should be in your school library or in the local public library.

Is your school board considering year-round classes? Is the board of county commissioners considering areas for a new landfill? Is the city council debating what to do about noise complaints? As you watch the television news, read the newspaper, or hear discussions about local government you will notice issues that affect you. This book can help you understand the ways local governments make decisions about those issues and your responsibilities and opportunities for participating in local government.

People live near one another for many reasons: to conduct business, to live near their work, and to enjoy the company of others, for example. There are many advantages to living in cities and towns, but living there also creates public problems—problems that affect the community at large.

One such problem is water supply. When houses are close together, individual wells for each house are likely to become contaminated unless there is a public sewer system or other provision for safe disposal of wastes. Moreover, private wells may not provide enough water for fighting fires. Fire threatens an entire community when houses are close enough that fire can easily spread from one house to others. Similarly, noise becomes a public problem when people live close enough together to be bothered by the sounds others make.

These houses in Wilmington were built when Wilmington was North Carolina's largest city. Like most houses in cities and towns, they were built close together.

Municipal governments have been established so that the people living in each place can deal with problems they face as a community. In North Carolina, municipal governments are called cities, towns, or (in a few cases) villages. In this state, these terms carry no special legal meaning. All three terms refer to a municipality created by the state and authorized to make decisions for a community and to carry out the policies and programs that have been approved. (In common usage, "towns" are often thought of as smaller than "cities," but that is not always true. The Town of Cary and the Town of Chapel Hill, for example, each have about 40,000 residents, and the cities of Claremont and High Shoals each have fewer than 1,000 residents.) North Carolina law establishes the powers and responsibilities for each municipality.

THE DEVELOPMENT OF TOWNS AND CITIES IN NORTH CAROLINA

European settlers established the first municipal governments in North Carolina in the early 1700s. Although they encountered Native American villages and sometimes built their own towns on the same sites, the Europeans established municipal governments based on English models. Each town was an independent municipality authorized under English, and later North Carolina, law.

Early North Carolina towns maintained public wells, established volunteer fire departments, and set up town watches to keep the peace. For example, the commissioners of Newbern (as it was then spelled) detailed the duties of the town watch in 1794 as follows:

> The gentlemen on watch are to use their best endeavours to prevent house breaking, and thieving, of every kind, and to seize and secure every person found committing, or attempting to commit any such offenses . . . .
>
> The watch will take up all suspicious and disorderly persons, who may be found in or strolling about the streets, after nine o'clock at night . . . .
>
> On discovering any danger by fire, one of the watch will immediately ring the church bell, one other of them will then inform the person, who has care of the water engine, and the others are to alarm the persons near where the greatest danger appears, and use their utmost endeavours, to assist those in distress.

By 1800 there were more than a dozen towns in North Carolina, but only four (Edenton, Fayetteville, New Bern, and Wilmington) had populations of 1,000 or more. North Carolina was a rural, agricultural state, and few people lived in cities or towns. The state remained largely rural throughout the nineteenth century. In 1850 Wilmington, the state's major port, was the only

About 1880, the Eagle Hotel in Asheville welcomed travelers who arrived by stagecoach.

town with more than 5,000 residents. Wilmington reached 10,000 in 1870. Asheville, Charlotte, and Raleigh each had more than 10,000 residents by 1880.

In the mid-nineteenth century, the North Carolina General Assembly (the state legislature) revised the laws regarding municipalities. Under an act passed in 1855, all municipalities were given the same powers. They could tax real estate, liquor dealers, tickets to shows, dogs, and freely roaming hogs, horses and cattle. They could appoint a town constable, regulate public markets, prevent public nuisances, protect public health, keep streets and bridges in repair, and regulate the quality and weight of loaves of bread baked for sale. As time passed, the General Assembly gave additional authority to individual municipalities and groups of municipalities. As a result, each North Carolina city or town may have a

Water supply to Raleigh residents improved with the construction of this water tower in 1887.

somewhat different set of powers and responsibilities.

Population growth brought the need for new municipal powers and responsibilities. Bigger towns created new problems for municipal governments. For example, adequate supplies of safe drinking water became a problem as cities became larger and more densely populated. The General Assembly established the State Board of Health in 1877, and one of its initial concerns was the threat of "enteric" diseases in the state's cities and towns. ("Enteric" diseases are intestinal infections. Typhoid and other enteric diseases are caused by bacteria that live in water. They are spread by water which has been contaminated with human wastes.)

To help prevent disease, Asheville built a system to supply filtered water to its residents in 1884. Water from the Swannanoa River was pumped four miles from the filtration plant to the city. The year after it was built, the State Board of Health reported that Asheville's new municipal water supply was the safest in the state and that there had been "a marked decrease in typhoid and other enteric diseases" in Asheville.

Not everyone in Asheville benefited from the new system, however. Although the city owned and operated the water-supply system, it charged twenty-five cents per thousand gallons of water. That was expensive for workers who supported their families on an average income of about $750 per year. Asheville city water was, therefore, "not in general use among the poorer classes," according to the Board of Health report.

In fact, Asheville's water rates were lower than those in many other cities. Unlike Asheville, most North Carolina city governments did not operate water systems. Instead private companies supplied water to city residents. In Charlotte, the private water company charged fifty cents per thousand gallons, and in Raleigh, the water company charged forty cents per thousand gallons. Many people could not afford to buy water at those

Raleigh firefighters were unable to prevent the loss of this hotel in 1928, but they kept the fire from destroying the city's growing business district.

rates. They continued to rely on unsanitary sources of water. Water supply, like many other services, did not become a municipal responsibility in many cities and towns until the twentieth century.

During the early years of the twentieth century, North Carolina towns and cities grew rapidly. By 1920, twenty percent of the state's 2.5 million people lived in municipalities. More cities and towns paved their streets as automobiles became common. They also set up full-time police and fire departments and adopted

Table 2.1
Distribution of Municipalities, 1990

Population of Municipality	Number of Municipalities of This Size	Total Population in Municipalities of This Size
Fewer than 2,500	354	297,501
2,500 to 9,999	107	492,186
10,000 to 49,999	40	851,251
50,000 or more	10	1,384,562
All cities and towns	511	3,025,500

Source: 1990 United States Census

building codes to regulate construction and reduce hazards to health and safety. Cities and towns bought private water and sewer companies during this period or started their own systems to make these services more widely available to their residents. A number of cities even started their own electric utilities to bring electricity to their communities.

Urban growth continued throughout the twentieth century. Municipal services continued to expand to meet the needs of the state's growing urban population. By 1990 almost all cities and towns had public water and sewer systems, paved streets, and police and fire protection. Other services such as garbage collection, parks, and recreation programs became increasingly common in municipalities throughout the state.

By 1990, Charlotte had almost 400,000 residents, Raleigh had more than 200,000, and Durham, Greensboro and Winston-Salem each had well over 100,000. Most North Carolina cities and towns continue to be small places, however. As Table 2.1 shows, only fifty North Carolina cities and towns had 10,000 residents or more in 1990.

HOW MUNICIPALITIES ARE CREATED

Corporation—
a group of persons formed by law to act as a single body.

Contract—
an agreement made between two or more people or organizations.

Sue—
to ask a court to act against a person or organization to prevent or pay for damage by that person or organization.

Liability—
the extent to which people can be assessed damages because of mistakes.

State government establishes cities and towns as municipal **corporations**. Like private corporations, municipal corporations can own property, enter **contracts**, and be **sued**. The owners of a corporation give responsibility for running the corporation to a board. The board acts on behalf of the owners in deciding what the corporation should do. A municipality's "owners"—the citizens of the jurisdiction—elect a board which is responsible for running the municipality. A citizen's **liability** for municipal debts is limited to the amount of tax owed to the municipality.

Municipal corporations differ from private corporations in important ways. For one thing, citizens become the "owners" of a municipal corporation simply by living within the municipality's jurisdiction. They do not buy the corporation's stock the way owners of a private, for-profit corporation do. Municipal corporations also have different powers than private corporations. Private corporations can engage in any legal activity they choose. North Carolina municipalities can engage only in those activities for which the General Assembly has given its permission, and the General Assembly may change municipal authority as it wishes. For example, the legislature might remove a city's authority to license taxi cabs or to operate swimming pools, and that city could then no longer carry out the activity. At the same time, municipal corporations are governments, and therefore they are given authority to make and enforce laws and to **levy** taxes.

The creation of a new city or town is called **incorporation**. Cities and towns must be incorporated by act of the General Assembly. The General Assembly may require the approval of the voters of the new municipality, but it does not need to do so. Incorporation includes defining the geographic boundaries of the new municipality and approving its **charter**, the rules under which it conducts its business.

A new city or town is generally incorporated after the development of a settlement in the area. Some towns grew up around county courthouses and were then incorporated. Others—like Ahoskie, Carrboro, and Durham—developed around mills or railway stations. The town of Princeville was incorporated by the General Assembly in 1885, twenty years after it was settled as a freedmen's camp by former slaves at the end of the Civil War. People ask for incorporation because they want to have a local government. They want public services, a means for providing public order and improving the community, and the right to participate in making local decisions.

Levy—
to impose a tax by law.

Incorporation—
the legal process of creating a new corporation.

Charter—
the document defining how a city or town is to be governed and giving it legal authority to act as a local government.

Archdale: The Growth of a City

During the 1960s a number of new houses were built in northwest Randolph County, just a few miles south of High Point. As the number of houses and businesses in the area increased, people in the area began to realize that a water-supply system was needed to provide safe drinking water. At the same time, many were opposed to becoming part of High Point. They wanted "self-rule," as one resident put it. That is, they wanted to govern how their community would grow and develop.

In 1969 the community was incorporated as Archdale. The city charter created a six-member council (two members from each of three wards) and a popularly elected mayor. The new city had only one employee, a clerk. The first service the city provided was garbage collection. The council hired a private company to collect the residents' trash and garbage.

In 1974 the voters of Archdale approved borrowing money to construct a water system for the city. By the end of 1976, Archdale residents were getting their water from a public water system. A public works department was in place to operate the water system and repair city streets.

In 1978 the Archdale police department was organized. (Before that time, law enforcement in Archdale was provided by the Randolph County sheriff's department.) The next year, the city opened its first park. Soon the city built a senior citizens' center in the park.

In 1984 Archdale built a sewer system to replace the septic tanks at existing houses and make development possible on land where septic tanks could not be used at all.

In twenty years, Archdale had changed a great deal. When it was incorporated it had about 2,000 residents and no city services. In the next twenty years it grew to about 7,000 residents. More businesses and several manufacturing companies also located in the city. The council hired a city manager to coordinate the city's operations. By 1992, 39 city employees were serving Archdale residents and businesses with water and sewer service, garbage collection, city police protection, city streets, and a city park and senior-citizen center.

The extension of municipal boundaries is called **annexation**. When territory is annexed to a city or town, that territory comes within the municipality's jurisdiction and its residents become part of the town's population. Voters in the annexed territory automatically become eligible to vote in the municipality's elections, and the municipality must provide its services to the new residents. Cities and towns may annex territory through an act of the General Assembly, by petition of the owners of the property to be annexed, or by **ordinance**. Annexation by ordinance usually requires that the territory is adjacent to the municipality and that it has already reached a certain level of urban development. Also, the municipality has to show that it will provide its services to the annexed territory.

In addition to following its own charter, each North Carolina municipality must also obey state laws and regulations. Some laws apply to all cities or towns of a certain size. These general laws provide most of the authority to act for North Carolina municipalities. However, sometimes a city wants to do something not authorized by general law or by its charter. Often in such cases the city asks the General Assembly to approve a **local act**. By custom, the General Assembly approves local acts which are favored by all of the representatives to the General Assembly from the jurisdiction that requests the local act.

GOVERNING CITIES AND TOWNS

Each municipality has its own governing board, elected by citizens of the city or town. Like the state legislature, a local governing board represents the people of the jurisdiction and has the authority to act for them. In many North Carolina cities and towns, the governing board is called the council, although "board of commis-

In the News . . .

As of Monday, town's a little bigger

By Janice Roy

As of midnight, the Town of Troy grew by 32 acres.

That area was annexed by the town during their regular meeting, after an annexation request was brought to the town by First Wesleyan Church.

According to Troy Mayor Roy Maness, the church asked that their land be annexed before the building of additional apartments for the elderly.

Matt Bernhardt, Troy town manager, explained that the apartments will be hooked onto the town's water and sewer system. "Our ordinances require that before someone can hook on to our system that they be within the town limits," he noted. "The first phase of the Wesleyan Home project is already within the town limits."

-reprinted from
Montgomery Herald
September 18, 1991

sioners" or "board of aldermen" are also names for municipal governing boards.

Regardless of whether they are called council members, commissioners, or aldermen, the members of the governing board make official decisions for the city. The governing board establishes local tax rates and adopts a budget which indicates how the city will spend its money. The governing board sets policies for municipal services, passes ordinances to regulate behavior, and enters into agreements on behalf of the municipality.

The voters also elect a mayor in most North Carolina cities and towns. In some places, however, the mayor is elected by the governing board. The mayor presides over the governing board and is typically the chief spokesperson for the municipality. In some small towns the mayor is also informally the chief administrator for the town. In most North Carolina municipalities, however, the mayor has no day-to-day responsibilities for administration.

Except for the smaller towns, North Carolina municipalities hire a professional manager (or administrator) to serve as chief executive. Under the **council-manager plan**, the manager is responsible for carrying out the council's policies and for running city government. The city (or town) manager is responsible for hiring and firing municipal employees, for coordinating their work, for advising the council on policy issues, for proposing a municipal budget, and for reporting to the council on municipal

Council-manager plan—
an arrangement for local government in which the elected legislature hires a professional executive to direct government activities.

Rocky Mount Mayor Fred Turnage (right) swears in newly elected council members Jimmie Armstrong, Helen Gay, and William Broughton.

activities. The manager "serves at the pleasure of the council." That means the council can fire the manager whenever a majority of the council decide they want a new manager. A manager must work closely with the council in developing policies for the city and with city employees in seeing that city policies are carried out.

Many small municipalities do not have a manager. Where there is no manager, the governing board participates more directly in administering the town's business. The board hires and directs town employees and administers the town together, as a committee.

Municipal employees do much of the work of city and town governments. City **personnel** include police officers, firefighters, water treatment plant operators, recreation supervisors, or others who provide services directly to city residents. Their work is supported by other city personnel: accountants, clerks, engineers, lawyers, secretaries, and a variety of other staff. These employees provide expert advice, train employees, pay bills, prepare reports, keep records, and do the many other things it takes to conduct a city's business. In 1990 more than 36,000 people worked for city and town governments in North Carolina.

City personnel are organized into departments. Each department specializes in a particular service, such as police work, fire protection, water supply, or recreation. Typically, the city manager selects department heads. They work with the city manager in planning and coordinating the activities of employees in their departments. In many cities, the manager relies on department

Personnel—

the people who work for a government, company, or other organization.

The Council-Manager Plan

The council-manager plan was developed in the United States to provide skilled professional administration for city government. In 1913, Hickory was one of the first cities in the entire country to hire a professional manager. Other North Carolina cities and towns soon followed.

Counties experimented with the plan during the 1920's. In 1929 Robeson County was the first in the nation to adopt the plan and keep using it. Durham County followed in 1930.

Today, North Carolina is one of the states that makes the most use of the council-manager plan of local government.

Most city and county managers are college graduates who have specialized education in public management. Many have graduate degrees—usually the Master of Public Administration degree. Most belong to the International City/County Management Association (ICMA). The ICMA provides professional assistance and continuing education for managers. It also has a Code of Ethics, which emphasizes the public-service values professional managers follow.

City/county managers are experts in planning and coordinating local government services. Their Code of Ethics calls on them to use their expertise for the entire community and to stay out of local politics, including elections for local officials. Professional managers help the elected board plan programs and services for the jurisdiction and are responsible for day-to-day administration of city government. Final responsibility for deciding on local policies rests with the elected board.

an interview with
Frank Cope
Town Administrator
Murfreesboro, NC

There are lots of benefits to working for a small town. Here in Murfreesboro, people know the mayor, the council, and me, and they have a solid grasp of what's going on in town. Even though I'm originally from Raleigh, people have made me feel very comfortable here, and they appreciate what I do.

One thing I like about my job is that I get to follow projects from start to finish—I see things getting done. One of the most rewarding projects I manage is a Community Development Block Grant from the federal government. We're using the funds to revitalize 23 homes on the edge of town. We're paving the street, weatherproofing and repairing roofs on the houses, and getting running water and sewer to all the residents. Twenty years from now, I can point to a project like that and be proud of what we accomplished.

Other projects happen behind the scenes, but they're just as important. When something needs to be done, it's my job to gather all the information and come up with as many options as possible, so the council can choose the best one. For example, we just had the inside of our water tank repainted. It sounds like a minor thing, but it has to be done. Otherwise the water gets rusty from corrosion on the inside of the tank. From talking to the engineers on the project, I learned a lot about the kinds of paint you can use in a water tank (NOT lead-based), the techniques for blasting off the old paint, and the proper temperature you need for the new paint to adhere to the metal. If you don't apply the paint right, it peels

off in sheets after a few years and gets into people's drinking water. I decided we should pay whatever it took to have the job done right. The project cost $60,000, but it was worth it.

If our water-supply system quit working, you'd notice as soon as you got up in the morning. The most important thing I do as a manager is make sure that we have clean, safe water. Solid waste and recycling are also big issues for our town. Our landfill is running out of room, and we're trying to select a new site. If we can get people to start recycling, we can make the new landfill last for twenty years.

Individuals can make a huge difference in local government. There are lots of things young people can do to help make Murfreesboro run better. They can teach their parents to recycle, and they can set up recycling programs in the school. They can check their houses to make sure no toilets are broken or leaking—millions of gallons of water get wasted in North Carolina every year. They can help build town spirit through their school, and they can keep their eyes open for problems that need attention.

If you see a problem that needs town action, call the town hall and let your officials know. The people who work for the town live in your community. They're your neighbors. It's their job to listen—they work for you.

—interviewed by
Roger Schlegel

heads and/or a personnel department to recruit applicants for city jobs, screen job candidates, and hire new employees. Department heads organize and supervise the employees in their departments.

The people who live in a city or town also play an important role in providing municipal services. Volunteers help supervise recreation programs, organize recycling, and even fight fires. Citizen advisory committees, boards, and commissions help city councils and city employees review and plan programs. Individual citizens influence city policies through petitions, public hearings, and conversations with city officials. Residents also help carry out city programs. They sort their trash for recycling. They call police or fire departments to report dangerous situations. Many municipal services cannot be provided effectively without the active cooperation of residents.

Municipal governments help people make their communities better places to live. They provide services to make life safer, healthier, and happier for the people who live there. They offer incentives for improving the appearance and economy of their community. They make and enforce laws to deal with public problems.

Youngsville police officers stop to talk to residents.

3 North Carolina Counties

No matter where you live in North Carolina, you live in a county and have a county government. Unlike municipalities, counties were not established to deal with the specific problems of living close together. Rather, counties were created to provide basic services that are important to people whether they live in rural or urban areas.

When you think of county government, the first image that comes to mind might be the courthouse. The county's central offices are usually located in the courthouse. Official records of births, deaths, marriages, divorces, and property—sometimes stretching back hundreds of years—are maintained there. But county government does not stop at the courthouse steps. Counties operate facilities ranging from health care clinics to jails.

There are two kinds of services that counties provide. Just as all cars come with standard equipment and can also have optional equipment added, counties provide some standard services and can also offer optional services. The standard services must be provided under state law. Because the state requires them, they are called **mandated services**. Part of the reason that the General Assembly has divided the state into counties is to ensure that every resident of North Carolina will have easier access to mandated

Mandated service—a program which local governments must provide because of requirements from state or federal government.

Chowan County's courthouse, built in 1767, is the state's oldest courthouse still in use.

services through his or her county government. In this way, you might think of your county as a "branch office" of the state government.

But counties do more than carry out state requirements. Like cities and towns, counties are a special kind of corporation, with the power to own property, to enter contracts, and to levy taxes. As local governments, counties have authority to regulate certain behavior (development of land or disposal of trash, for example), to encourage county improvement, and even to provide many of the same services cities and towns provide. In addition to the mandated services they must provide, most counties also adopt regulations, encourage community improvement, and provide other services. Depending on the needs of the area and the requests of local citizens, county officials may decide to provide various **optional services**. For example, with an increasing number of people living outside the boundaries of cities and towns, such optional services as water and sewers or parks and recreation are becoming more popular choices for counties.

Who gets county services? It depends. Most county services are available to all county residents, whether they live inside or outside a city or town. However, some services may be provided only to the **unincorporated** part of the county (the area outside city or town limits). For example, because most municipalities have their own police department, the county sheriff (or county police in Gaston and Mecklenburg counties) usually provides police patrol and criminal investigation only in unincorporated areas.

Optional service—
a program that a government decides to provide to meet the needs or requests of its residents.

Unincorporated—
the part of a county outside the cities and towns in that county.

Many counties now make parks available to their residents.

In this chapter, you will see how North Carolina's 100 county governments developed and how they are organized. You will also take a look at services provided only by counties. Chapter four will discuss other services that may be provided by either municipalities or counties.

THE DEVELOPMENT OF NORTH CAROLINA COUNTIES

North Carolinians are especially proud of their counties and often identify themselves by the county where they live. Although county governments are similar in many ways, each county has a distinct personality that reflects the character and history of the people who live there.

Counties were a key part of colonial government in North Carolina. As British control and European settlement extended westward from the coast, the British authorities set up new counties to provide government for the colonists. The governor of the colony appointed justices of the peace in each county. The justices served as both the court and the administrators for the county. The justices of the peace appointed constables to enforce the law. They appointed a sheriff to collect taxes, and they appointed wardens to care for the poor. The justices also appointed a surveyor to mark land boundaries and a register of deeds to keep property records. Establishing land boundaries and maintaining records of property were very important to the farmers and planters who settled the colony. Having government officials nearby was especially important before the development of modern transportation, because it could take many hours to travel only a few miles.

There were 35 counties in North Carolina when the state

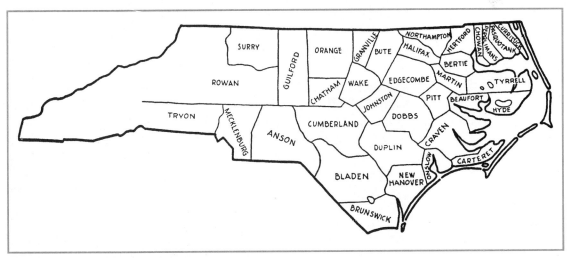

Map 3.1 North Carolina counties in 1775.

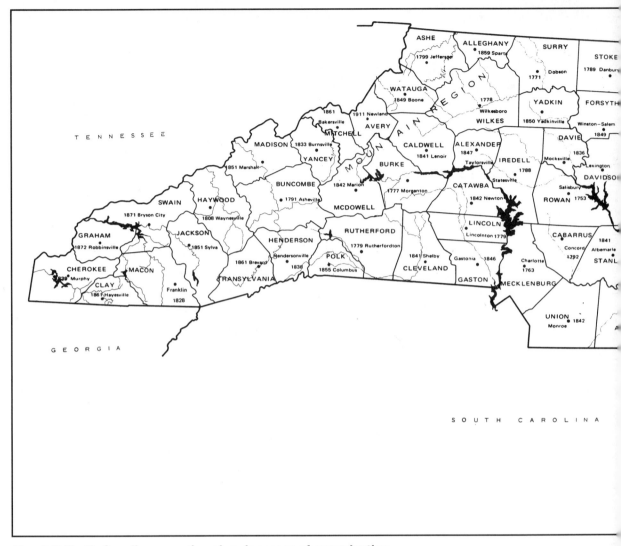

Map 3.2 North Carolina counties showing year of organization.

declared its independence from Great Britain in 1776. After independence North Carolina state government continued to use counties to organize local citizens and provide basic government throughout the state. The General Assembly also continued to create new counties to bring government closer to the people. By 1800 there were 65 counties and by 1900 there were 97. In the twentieth century only three additional counties were created. The last one was created in 1912, bringing the total to 100.

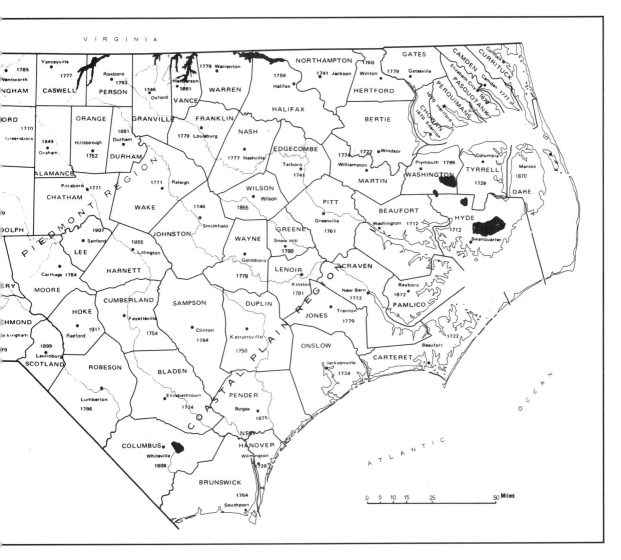

EACH COUNTY IS DIFFERENT

There is no "typical" North Carolina county. North Carolina's 100 counties are diverse. In area, they range from Chowan County (173 square miles) to Robeson County (949 square miles). The population differences are even greater. In 1990, Tyrrell County had the smallest population (3,856 residents) and Mecklenburg County the largest (511,433 residents). Population density varies widely across counties, too. Hyde County had only about nine people per square mile in 1990, whereas Mecklenburg County had 970 people per square mile.

The land in the western part of the state is mountainous. Many of the **mountain counties** are heavily forested. The land is a flat

Mountain counties—the western region of North Carolina, extending eastward from the Tennessee border to the eastern boundaries of Alleghany, Wilkes, Caldwell, Burke, and Rutherford counties. This region includes 23 counties.

coastal plain in the eastern part of the state. Some counties on the coastal plain are also heavily forested, but many are rich agricultural areas with many highly productive farms. Most of the mountain and coastal plain counties are **rural**. Agriculture and forestry are important economic activities in both parts of the state. Tourism is also important to the economy of the mountains and the coast. Fishing is important along the coast. There are few **urban** counties in either area. Only Buncombe (Asheville) in the mountains and Cumberland (Fayetteville) and New Hanover (Wilmington) on the coastal plain are predominantly urban and had more than 250 people per square mile in 1990.

The **piedmont**, in the central part of the state, is an area of rolling hills. North Carolina's biggest cities are in the piedmont, and several piedmont counties are mostly urban. Nine piedmont counties have more than 250 people per square mile (Alamance, Cabarrus, Catawba, Durham, Forsyth, Gaston, Guilford, Mecklenburg, and Wake). However, most piedmont counties are largely rural. Farming is a more important part of the economy in the eastern piedmont counties than in the western piedmont counties. Manufacturing (especially textiles, clothing, and furniture) is particularly important in the western piedmont counties, where even many rural counties have a considerable amount of industry.

COUNTIES RESPOND TO POPULATION CHANGES

Population change greatly affects county governments. A change in the number of residents means a change in the demand for services as well as a change in the amount of taxes needed to pay for those services. Since 1950 some North Carolina counties have become more densely populated, others have maintained their population, and still others have lost population. Overall, the population of the state increased by 63 percent from 1950 to 1990, but most of that increase was concentrated in about half of the state's counties. Map 3.3 shows how each county's population changed during that time.

Although the urban population in North Carolina has grown much more rapidly than the rural population, the state is still mostly rural. Even in 1990, more than half of all North Carolina residents lived outside municipalities. As Figure 3.1 shows, only forty-five percent of the state's 6.6 million people lived in cities, towns, or villages in 1990.

New Residents, New Jobs

Three kinds of development have contributed most to population growth during the second half of the twentieth century. New

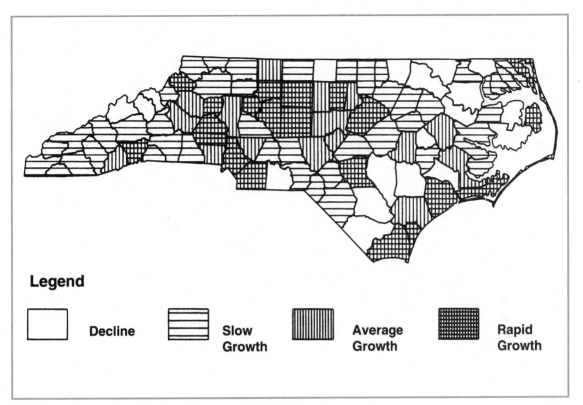

Map 3.3 County Population changes, 1950-1990.

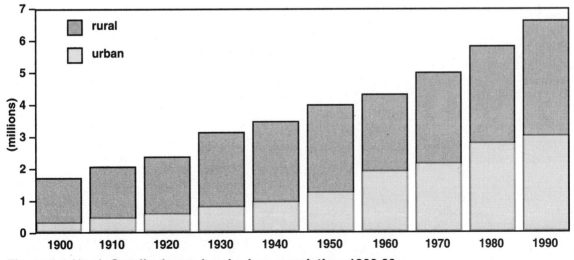

Figure 3.1 North Carolina's rural and urban population, 1900-90.

Housing developments dot the North Carolina countryside, creating some of the same problems living close together brings about in cities and towns. Many counties have begun providing water, sewers, and other "city" services to housing developments in unincorporated areas.

and rapidly expanding businesses created jobs and led to increased population in some counties. Much of this kind of growth occurred in the piedmont, with Mecklenburg and Wake counties having the greatest population increase. Military base development contributed much to the population growth in some coastal plain counties, especially Cumberland (Fort Bragg) and Onslow (Camp LeJeune). Resort and retirement community developments also contributed to major population growth in several counties, particularly in the mountains (Henderson, Watauga) and at the beach (Brunswick, Currituck, Dare).

In each case, additional jobs were also created as people moved into these developing counties. Whether they came to take jobs created by expanding businesses, to serve on military bases, or to retire, new residents needed housing, food, clothing, banking, and other goods and services. This need led to the expansion of other businesses and to the creation of additional jobs.

As a result of the development of new jobs, people in counties with population growth generally have higher incomes than those who live in counties with little or no population growth.

More People, More Services

Population growth creates the need for additional government services. Not only are there more people to be served, but the kinds of services needed may also change as the population increases. For example, housing developments outside city limits may still require public water and sewer systems to protect the public health. Thus, county government might need to begin providing water and sewer services in unincorporated areas. New school buildings and other public facilities are also needed as the population increases. County governments must pay for these new facilities and hire new employees to serve their larger population.

The Special Needs of Counties That Have Not Grown

Not all counties experience population growth at the same time. In North Carolina many counties that are primarily agricultural had little population growth or even lost population in the second half of the twentieth century. Machines replaced people for many farming operations during this period. In 1947, forty-two percent of North Carolinians worked in agriculture. By 1987, only three percent of North Carolinians worked in agriculture. In some rural counties, manufacturing or tourist jobs replaced agricultural jobs. In other counties, however, there were few new jobs to replace those lost on the farms. These are the counties that lost population or had little population growth. These are also the counties where **per capita** income is the lowest.

Per capita— for each person.

Counties with constant or declining population often have special problems. High unemployment and low wages mean that a larger proportion of the population needs financial assistance and health care from the county government. At the same time, poorer people pay fewer taxes. A county with a low per capita income may well have trouble raising funds to assist its needy residents.

In the News . . .

Jail almost full despite expansion

By Bettie Fennell

Despite an expansion that added 83 beds this summer, the New Hanover County Jail is already nearing capacity.

To relieve overcrowding, the county agreed to a $1.2 million expansion of the Law Enforcement Center, part of which came from federal funds. The county began using the extra beds August 1, increasing the number of beds to 209. Another 92 beds are available at an annex on Division Drive, which houses less violent prisoners, such as those convicted of driving while impaired.

Friday, only five beds were empty at the jail, said Sheriff Joe McQueen.

"That was the closest we've been" since the expansion was opened, said Capt. Robert E. Spell.

—adapted from
The Morning Star
September 15, 1992

Local voters in North Carolina could not select their own county officials until after the Civil War. Up until that time the state appointed county officials. The North Carolina Constitution of 1868 provided for the election of the sheriff, the coroner, the register of deeds, the clerk of court, the surveyor, and the treasurer. Under the 1868 constitution, voters in each county also began to elect a board of county commissioners. The board of county commissioners replaced appointed justices of the peace as officers of general government for the county. These county boards were responsible for the county's finances, including setting its tax rates.

Today, voters in each North Carolina county elect a board of county commissioners, a sheriff, a register of deeds, and a clerk of court. The clerk of court is no longer an office of county government, however. The General Assembly consolidated all county courts into a state-wide court system, and the clerk, although elected by the county's voters, is an employee of the state courts. Judges and district attorneys are elected by judicial districts. Some judicial districts include only a single county, but in many cases they include several counties. Regardless of the size of the judicial district, however, judges and district attorneys are state officials, not county officials. A few counties still elect a coroner, but the General Assembly has reassigned legal responsibility for determining cause of death to the medical examiner. Voters also elect members of the local school board, which may cover an entire county, but sometimes includes only a part of a county. Thus, the county commissioners, the sheriff, and the register of deeds are the only county officials elected by voters in each of the 100 counties.

The Board of County Commissioners

The board of county commissioners has general responsibility for county government. Unlike a city or town governing board, however, the board of county commissioners shares authority for setting county policy with other officials—state officials, the sheriff, the register of deeds, and independent county boards. The General Assembly and various state agencies are often directly involved in setting policy for county governments through mandates that require the county to provide certain services or follow specific procedures. As elected officials, the sheriff and the register of deeds have authority independent of the board of county commissioners and may set policies for their departments. Furthermore, state law provides for separate boards with responsibility for alcoholic beverage control, education, elections, health, mental health, and social services policy.

Independent Boards

The independent boards that have responsibility for helping set local policy in North Carolina counties appoint directors for their agencies and make local policies regarding agency operations. Smaller counties may join together in a single health district or mental health area, with boards made up of representatives from each of the participating counties. Larger counties typically have their own health and mental health boards. In counties where alcoholic beverages may be sold, an Alcoholic Beverage Control (ABC) Board controls ABC stores in the county.

County social services boards hire a director for the county department of social services and advise the director on program needs and budget requests. Because many social service programs are funded by the United States government, federal and state regulations set much of the policy for social services delivered by counties.

The county elections board sets policies for operations of local voter registration and elections and selects an elections supervisor to manage those operations.

Most North Carolina counties have a single, county-wide administrative unit for public schools, although some counties have more than one school system. Except for a few city school districts with appointed boards of education, the voters of each district elect the board of education for each school unit.

None of the independent boards has the authority to levy taxes. County funds to support these services must be raised by the board of county commissioners. All of the independent boards must also have their budgets approved by the board of county commissioners. The responsibility for financing operations and the power to control **expenditures** gives the board of county commissioners the ability to coordinate county policy for the services with independent boards. Because it raises and **allocates** county funds, the board of county commissioners has the potential to influence all government programs that depend on county money, including even the schools, which operate as separate administrative units.

Expenditures—
money spent.

Allocate—
to set aside money for a specific purpose.

The County Manager

In nearly all North Carolina counties, the board of county commissioners hires a manager. The county manager directs the general operations of county government. He or she has the authority to hire and to fire personnel in departments directly under the authority of the board of commissioners. The county manager does not have the authority to hire or to fire personnel responsible to an independently elected official (sheriff, register of deeds) or

an interview with
Richard Y. Stevens
Wake County Manager
Raleigh, NC

Wake County Manager Richard Stevens

County management is more about persuading than about directing. You can't just say, "Pave this road" and get it paved or "Change this stop light" and get it changed. In county government, you have to collaborate with other independent divisions of government—local, state, and federal—and with other elected groups, citizen groups, and advisory groups in order to get anything done. Both city and county managers are responsible for carrying out the intent of their governing bodies with respect to the types and extent of government services provided, but city managers have more direct control over service areas.

This county is blessed with a board of commissioners who are policy makers. This means that they delegate the day-to-day responsibility for governing to the staff. They do not dwell on details of administration or day-to-day operations at all. It's a policy-oriented board.

Counties deal with services that are important to people. Wake County, like most counties, has a major responsibility for funding education. State and federal governments have also given the county responsibility to manage human and social services. Beyond that, the county is responsible for running a large library program, for law enforcement and jail (sheriff's department), and for an array of regulatory programs in zoning, permitting, solid waste disposal, and environmental issues. More recently the county has become involved in things like historic preservation, parks and recreation, cultural programs, and sporting events. Wake County is an urban county providing many city-like services,

but our major issues and responsibilities continue to be education, human services, and the quality of life.

Because of what government is all about and what it does, be involved in government. Vote. Communicate with elected officials if you're not satisfied with what's going on. It may be a phone call. It may be a letter. It may be running into them on the street corner or grocery store or sitting next to them in church or the library. Local government officials are available. We are responsive to citizens—and by *we*, I mean staff and elected officials. Ask questions. Go to a council or commission meeting. Keep challenging your local officials on issues as students. They will hear you!

— interviewed by
Marcy Onieal

personnel that state law places under the state personnel system or an independent board (alcoholic beverage control, education, elections, health, social services). The county manager also prepares a budget for the county and manages the county's expenditures. He or she also reports to the board of commissioners on county government operations and on public problems facing the county. The county manager serves at the pleasure of the board of county commissioners.

SERVICES PROVIDED BY COUNTY GOVERNMENTS

North Carolina counties provide many essential services for all North Carolina residents. The county register of deeds maintains legal records of all property transactions and of marriages, births, and deaths. The county board of elections registers voters and conducts elections. The county sheriff operates a jail to hold people awaiting trial and people convicted of minor crimes. Counties provide emergency medical services either through county departments or through support for volunteer emergency medical service (EMS) squads. Counties also have responsibility for social services, public health services, and mental health services. Funding the public schools is also a major county responsibility.

Social Services

North Carolina counties have important responsibilities for assisting people with low incomes and other social problems. County departments of social services help children through programs like foster care, adoption, and family counseling. They investigate suspected abuse of children and disabled adults. They offer services to help the elderly and the disabled live at home, and programs to help people prepare for new jobs. County departments of social services often work closely with religious and other charitable organizations in providing these services.

In providing some services, the county must follow very specific regulations. For example, counties must operate **Aid to Families with Dependent Children (AFDC)**, **Food Stamps**, and **Medicaid** programs according to strict federal regulations. Counties must follow these regulations in determining who is eligible to receive assistance from these programs and in organizing and operating their departments of social services to carry out the programs. In part, this is because counties pay only a part of AFDC, Food Stamps, and Medicaid costs. A majority of the funds for each of these programs comes from the U.S. government. To be eligible for funds from the U.S. government, states must have programs that meet federal requirements. Most of the fifty states use a

Aid to Families with Dependent Children (AFDC)— *financial aid to families that do not have enough money for basic needs, like housing and food. AFDC is a federal program, but is administered by county departments of social services in North Carolina.*

Food Stamps— *a program to help people with financial need buy food. The program issues vouchers to be used like money for purchasing food. This is a federal program, but is administered by county departments of social services in North Carolina.*

Medicaid— *a program designed to pay for medical care for people in financial need. This is a federal program, but is administered by county departments of social services in North Carolina.*

Fighting for your health

By Jerry Gentry

Most people know the Durham County Health Department only as the place to get septic tank permits, birth and death certificates, or flu shots.

They don't realize that that's where the warriors hang out, warriors fighting communicable diseases.

Their director, Dr. John Fletcher, is totally committed to protecting the public's health and enforcing all applicable laws of state and local origin. So, too, are his staff members. Clearly, he is proud of them. He doesn't look over their shoulders, he says, but he does expect them to produce for the 181,000 people in Durham county. And produce they do.

Durham had the state's first early-intervention AIDS program, and two Health Department programs have become models for North Carolina.

"I really trust my staff," he said. "I give them room to work. They develop their own plans and budgets. I'm responsible, but they have ownership of programs. That way you have commitment and good programs."

He administers a department of about 165 people with a $5.5 million budget and answers to an 11-member Board of Health appointed by the county commissioners.

Talk to him and you'll see, as I did, that this is a man of integrity, wit, and commitment.

Dr. Fletcher plans to retire (maybe) in the spring of 1996 and devote himself to the study of Greek and Hebrew. By that time, he will have handled the rabies outbreak he expects, the TB outbreak that's already upon us, the AIDS management programs in place, a new high-risk baby program—and who knows what else?

— adapted from
The Herald-Sun
August 31, 1992

department of state government to administer public assistance, but North Carolina is one of few states that chose to assign that responsibility to the counties. Still, the state (which also pays part of the cost) has to assure the U.S. government that federal requirements are being met. Strict regulation of county operations is one way to do that.

Another reason for strict regulation of public assistance programs is concern about welfare fraud. Many people believe that having very strict regulations will help ensure that only those who really need public assistance will receive these benefits. Others argue that too many regulations make it difficult for people to get the public assistance they need and drive up the cost for those who do receive benefits.

To provide greater flexibility in meeting people's needs for financial assistance, most North Carolina counties have established their own general assistance programs. These optional programs help people deal with emergencies and situations not covered by federal and state programs. The county social services board establishes the rules for general assistance in its county, and the board of county commissioners allocates county funds to pay for general assistance. Government programs do not cover all basic needs, however. Religious groups and other charitable organizations operate shelters for the homeless and for battered women, food banks and hot meals programs, clothing distribution centers, and other projects to meet the basic needs of those who cannot earn enough money to provide for themselves. Some of these charitable organizations also receive funding from county government to help them deliver specific social services.

Public Health

Local public health departments work to improve people's health in three ways: they remove health hazards from the environment; they educate people and give shots to prevent illness; and they care for those who are ill and cannot afford to pay for care. In North Carolina, each county is served by both a mental health department and a health department.

Whether it is organized for a single county or for two or more counties, each health department must meet certain state mandates. It must inspect restaurants, hotels, and other public accommodations in the county to be sure that the facilities and the food are safe. It must also collect information and report to the state about births, deaths, and communicable diseases in the county.

Local health departments also typically provide many other services. They have programs to prevent animals, such as mosquitoes and rats, from spreading human diseases. Many health depart-

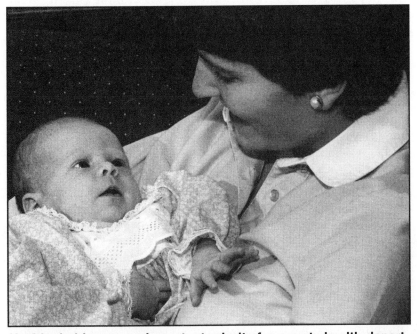

Healthy babies are an important priority for county health departments and social services departments because of both state mandates and local concern.

ments also enforce local sanitation ordinances for septic tanks or swimming pools and local animal-control ordinances. County nurses and health educators teach people about good nutrition and how to prevent illness. Most county health departments operate clinics to diagnose and treat illnesses and to provide health care for expectant mothers, infants, and children who cannot otherwise afford health care. County nurses also care for people in their homes and at school. They also give shots to prevent certain diseases.

Community-based treatment of mental illnesses, mental retardation, and the abuse of alcohol and other drugs are operated by the area mental health authority (either a single-county board or a multi-county board). These services are another important part of each county's responsibilities for public health education and care.

Public Schools

In North Carolina, the public schools are both a state and a local responsibility. The state pays teachers' basic salaries and establishes qualifications for teachers. Teachers are considered state employees. The state does not hire teachers, however. Teachers are hired by local school boards, and local school boards are also responsible for deciding to keep or to dismiss teachers.

The North Carolina State Board of Education establishes overall policies for the schools, including the minimum length of the school year, the content of the curriculum, and the textbooks that may be used. Local boards of education must meet the state's guidelines for school policy in all of their decisions about how the local schools will operate. Local school boards hire school administrators: principals, superintendents, and their assistants. Local school boards decide what texts to use and what courses to offer. They set the calendar for the local schools and decide on school attendance policies.

Local school boards also adopt a budget for operating the schools. Although teachers' basic salaries are paid by the state, most other costs of the schools are a local responsibility. These include buildings, furniture, and equipment; books and other supplies; maintenance; and utilities. Many local school systems also pay teachers a salary bonus. The local school board decides how much it needs to spend to support the local schools. Then it presents this budget to the board of county commissioners. The school board has no authority to tax. The county commissioners decide how much to spend to support local schools. In most counties, schools receive the largest share of county money. Sometimes there is considerable discussion between the school board and the commissioners about how much money the schools should receive.

Each local school board hires a superintendent to coordinate planning for the schools, to hire teachers and other school staff, to prepare and administer the budget, and to provide general administrative direction for the schools. Each school has a principal who has similar responsibilities for that school. In many parts of the state, schools are also beginning to involve teachers and parents more directly in helping plan for the school and in making decisions about how the school is run. Some schools also have advisory committees of people from local businesses and other members of the community.

The public schools have the responsibility of helping their students prepare for life. Some public-school programs help prepare students directly for work. Other programs help students prepare for college. All public-school programs should result in making students responsible citizens—people who take pride in their community and help make it a better place to live and work.

Public Facilities

Counties must also provide certain public facilities. Each county's board of county commissioners is required by the state to build and maintain a jail and to provide adequate office space for other mandated services. In addition, the board of county commission-

Sections of a new Robeson County jail are lifted into place. To save time and money, the cells for the jail were built in a factory and brought to the building site by truck.

ers is responsible for providing suitable space and equipment for the state's district and superior courts.

Mandates Change

When the state requires counties to provide a service, the county must carry out that mandate. Mandates change, however. The General Assembly has changed counties' service responsibilities many times over the years. For example, one early responsibility of county governments in North Carolina was the construction and maintenance of rural roads and bridges. During the 1930s, however, the General Assembly transferred all responsibility for rural roads and bridges to the state highway department, now the North Carolina Department of Transportation.

Counties get new responsibilities, too. In the late 1980s, the General Assembly passed laws requiring all counties to provide for the safe disposal of solid wastes produced in the county and to reduce by twenty-five percent the amount of waste going into landfills. This new mandate put all 100 counties in the business of managing solid waste. Many counties for the first time began programs to recycle, reuse, or compost solid wastes or to encourage people to create less waste material.

All of the mandated services are available to all county residents, whether they live in cities or towns or in the unincorporated part of the county.

Counties also provide many optional services to their residents. Some optional services—public libraries and parks and recreation programs, for example—are typically available to all county residents. Other services, such as rural water or sewer systems or rural fire departments, may be provided by county government only for unincorporated areas.

As we have seen, North Carolina county government is complex. The board of county commissioners has general responsibility for the county's finances and for many county services. However, state mandates, independently elected officials, and other independent boards also determine policy for many county-funded services. Counties are both local governments and divisions of state government. Counties are local governments in that they provide a government through which citizens can address local problems and opportunities. Counties are also a division of state government because they have to carry out many state programs that are mandated by North Carolina state law. Regardless of where you live in North Carolina, county government helps to shape your daily life.

Public Services

- You turn the handle on the faucet, and water flows into your glass.

- You put your trash out, and it is picked up and carried away.

- You play ball or swim in the pool at the park.

- You call the police or sheriff about a break-in at your house, and an officer comes to investigate.

Safe drinking water, regular trash collection, recreation opportunities, and police protection are among the many services provided by local governments. You and your family may use some of these services—water, for example—many times every day. Other services—trash collection or recreation—you may use only once or twice a week. Still other services—criminal investigations, for instance—you may use only rarely, but they are available whenever you need them.

Table 4.1 (on the next page) lists the major services that North Carolina city and county governments have authority to provide under state law. No one government provides all of the services on this list. As we saw in the last chapter, counties must provide certain mandated services. Except for the mandated services, municipalities and counties choose which services they will provide, depending on the needs and interests of their citizens. When a government provides a service, government

Fighting fires is one of the vital public services that local governments provide.

Table 4.1 Major Services and Programs Provided by Counties and Municipalities in North Carolina

The list below shows which local governments usually provide a service. Remember, not every government provides each service. Also, there are several exceptions. For example, a few cities have jails and a few counties have public transit.

A. Services Usually Provided by Counties Only

1. Community Colleges
2. Cooperative (agricultural) extension
3. Court facilities
4. Elections
5. Forest protection
6. Jails
7. Medical examiner
8. Mental health services
9. Public health services
10. Public schools
11. Register of deeds
12. Social services
13. Soil and water conservation
14. Youth detention facilities

B. Services Usually Provided by Both Municipalities and Counties

1. Airports
2. Ambulance service
3. Animal shelters
4. Art galleries and museums
5. Auditoriums/coliseums
6. Building inspection
7. Cable television regulation
8. Community appearance
9. Community and economic development
10. Emergency management
11. Environmental protection
12. Fire protection
13. Historic preservation
14. Human relations
15. Industrial development
16. Job training
17. Law enforcement
18. Libraries
19. National Guard
20. Open space and parks
21. Planning and zoning
22. Recreation programs
23. Rescue squads
24. Senior citizen programs
25. Sewer systems
26. Solid waste services
27. Storm drainage
28. Veterans' services
29. Water supply and protection

C. Services Usually Provided by Municipalities Only

1. Buses/public transit
2. Cemeteries
3. Electric systems
4. Gas systems
5. Public housing
6. Sidewalks
7. Street lighting
8. Streets
9. Traffic control
10. Urban development

officials use public money to pay for the service. They decide what kind of service will be produced, and they take responsibility for assuring that the service will meet the standards they set for it.

In this chapter you will go "behind the scenes" to see how a few public services are produced. You will look at water and sewer services, trash (solid waste) collection and disposal, recreation, and policing. These services are just examples of the many services local governments provide. Counties, cities, and towns also operate public libraries, provide fire protection, support hospitals, maintain animal shelters, and conduct many other public services.

Often local governments produce these services themselves. For example, they set up departments to operate water supply facilities, to collect trash, or to police the community. Sometimes, however, local governments hire a private business, a nonprofit organization, or another government to produce a service. Government hiring of a business to produce a public service is called **privatization**. The government buys the service from the business rather than hiring government employees to produce the service.

Privatization— government buying a service from a business instead of producing the service itself.

Regardless of who produces public services, however, government pays for them. Governments raise most of the money to pay for services through taxes. For some services, the local government charges users of the service to help cover the cost of providing the service. For example, most governments charge their customers for the water they use.

Many public services are directly helpful to customers—the people who use them. For example, you drink the water, get rid of

Public libraries make books available to young and old.

your trash, swim in the pool, or have a crime investigated. These services are called "user-focused" services.

But many of these services also benefit the community at large. Having a safe, abundant water supply protects everyone in the community from diseases spread by contaminated water and also supports firefighting. Safe, efficient waste collection and disposal helps keep the community healthy and attractive. Public recreation also supports a healthier, happier community. Criminal investigation helps protect the entire community from crime. Thus, public services benefit you both as an individual user and as a member of the community.

WATER SUPPLY

Public water systems have four parts: source, treatment, distribution, and wastewater treatment. Water is pumped from the source into a treatment plant. The water is treated to make it safe to drink. Then the water is pumped into storage tanks, from which it is distributed through pipes to the people who will use it. Finally, wastewater is treated. Controlling water pollution is important to assure a safe supply of drinking water. Wastewater can be a major source of water pollution. Sewage collection and treatment systems are essential to safe water supply systems.

Water Supply Sources

Wells are one important source of water in North Carolina. Wells tap into underground water. They allow water to be pumped out of the layers of sand, gravel, or porous rock, where it is trapped. In places where there are large pockets of underground water, wells can provide a steady source of water for public water systems. Rain and other water on the surface of the earth seeps down to replace the **ground water** that is pumped out. In rural areas where there is no public water system, each house may have its own well. Towns also use wells to supply public water systems where ground water is abundant.

Rivers and reservoirs are other important water sources for public water systems. North Carolina has many rivers, and frequent rainfall ensures that they flow all year long. Some cities located near a river simply pump their water from the river. Where there is no convenient river with enough water, reservoirs must be built to catch and hold rainwater until it is needed. Most of North Carolina's larger cities, and many smaller ones, depend on water from reservoirs. Water from rivers and reservoirs is called **surface water**. All of the land that drains into a reservoir is called the **watershed** for that reservoir. Watershed protection can reduce con-

Ground water—
water that collects underground.

Surface water—
water in lakes or streams.

Watershed—
an area that drains water into a stream or lake.

tamination of rivers and reservoirs, but surface water is still likely to be more contaminated than ground water.

Reservoirs are much more expensive water sources than either wells or rivers. Building a reservoir requires buying the land that will be flooded by the new lake and constructing a dam to contain the water. Engineers must first design a dam and map out the area the new lake will cover. Then the agency building the reservoir can begin to buy the land. Many reservoirs are built specifically to supply water. Some dams that provide water are built for other purposes, however. The federal government, working through the Army Corps of Engineers, builds reservoirs for flood control. Some private companies build reservoirs for electric power generation. If a city has to build its own reservoir, the cost of the reservoir is paid by the customers who use water. Thus, cities that must build reservoirs to ensure an adequate supply of water usually have higher water rates than cities that are able to get all the water they need from wells or rivers.

The most expensive method of supplying water is using sea water. Along the coast, a few communities take the salt out of sea water through a process called **desalinization**.

Water Treatment

The kind of treatment that water needs depends upon the **impurities** in it. Water from wells sometimes has almost no impurities. It has been filtered naturally as it collects below ground. On the other hand, underground water can become contaminated if harmful substances are buried nearby. To help prevent contamination of ground water, the federal government has passed several environmental protection laws. One law outlaws the discharge of dangerous chemicals into a stream or into the soil. Another requires landfills to be lined so that water cannot seep out of them and carry materials into the ground water. Still another law requires underground storage tanks (such as those for gasoline) to be rustproof so they will not leak.

Surface water picks up such things as the oil and grit from streets and parking lots, the fertilizer and pesticides from fields, trash or waste that is left exposed, and even soil particles. Therefore, surface water generally requires more treatment than well water. The first step in treating surface water is to filter it.

At the water treatment plant, filtering and sedimentation remove solid particles from the water. (Sedimentation involves adding chemicals to the water that cause the suspended solids to clump together and sink.) The water must next be treated chemically to kill harmful bacteria. Chlorine compounds are typically

Desalinization— the process by which the salt is taken out of sea water.

Impurities— materials that pollute or keep whatever they are in from being pure.

added to the water for this purpose. In many places, fluorine compounds are also added to the water to reduce tooth decay. Water plant operators must constantly monitor the water through each stage of treatment to be sure they are adding just the right amount of each of the chemicals they use.

Water Distribution

Treated water is pumped into elevated storage tanks so that it can flow through underground pipes to all the places it will be used. Each house, school, office building, store, or factory using water from the public water system is connected to the water distribution lines. Another expense in providing a public water supply is the construction of the water lines.

A meter at the point of connection measures how much water flows out of the line and into each customer's property. These meters are read periodically, and the customer is billed for the water that has passed through the meter.

Besides distributing water to users, the water lines provide another benefit. Fire hydrants connected to the lines give firefighters ready access to water used in fighting fires. Public water systems need to be designed to deliver enough water for fire fighting, as well as for residential, commercial, and industrial uses. A ready supply of water for fighting fires is an important community benefit of water supply systems.

Town employees replace insulation on a water line that runs beneath a bridge in Franklin.

Chapter 4

Samples of treated wastewater must be tested regularly to be sure the water is safe to release from the treatment plant.

Sewage Collection and Treatment

The liquid wastes from houses, schools, stores, offices, and factories are potentially dangerous. If they are not treated, these wastes can contaminate water with the chemicals or bacteria they carry. To avoid contaminating drinking water, hazardous chemicals, such as oil and many industrial and cleaning products, should not be poured on the ground or down the drain.

In some areas, drains go into **septic tanks** in which harmful bacteria are killed by natural processes. In these areas each house usually has its own septic tank. However, septic tanks cannot be used in densely populated areas or in areas where the soil will not readily absorb the water that has been treated in the tank. In these areas, wastewater flows into sewers, which carry it to a sewage treatment plant.

At the sewage treatment plant, chemical and biological processes eliminate harmful chemicals and bacteria from the wastewater and separate solids from the liquid wastes. The solid material separated from sewage is called **sludge**. Properly treated sludge is safe to use for fertilizer and is often recycled in that way. Properly treat-

Septic tank—
a container in which wastes are broken down by bacteria.

Sludge—
the solid material separated from sewage.

ed water is safe to release into rivers or lakes. This water is safe to drink and becomes a part of the water supply for residents farther downstream.

Public Water Systems

Most cities and towns operate their own water supply and wastewater systems. An increasing number of counties have also begun to operate water distribution and sewage treatment facilities in areas where wells and septic tanks cannot provide safe water and safe wastewater disposal. Some cities and counties cooperate with one another in producing water or sewage services. In a few parts of the state, special water and sewer agencies have been created by local governments to operate water and sewer facilities for the entire area. Examples include the Charlotte-Mecklenburg Utility District and the Orange Water and Sewer Authority. Other counties, such as Catawba, loan money to local municipalities so that they can extend water service to unincorporated areas.

SOLID WASTE MANAGEMENT

Everything you no longer want or need has to go somewhere. The solid wastes you generate—old newspapers, food scraps, used packaging, grass clippings—have to be disposed of safely. Chemicals from casually discarded trash can contaminate water. Garbage and trash also create a health hazard by providing a home for rats and other disease-bearing pests. Burning trash does not solve the problem of safe disposal because burning pollutes the air.

Local government helps solve the problem of safe disposal of solid waste. But safe (and low-cost) solid waste disposal also requires your cooperation and that of everyone in the community. The least expensive way to deal with waste is simply not to create it in the first place. Cutting out the use of packaging and disposable items, for example, can reduce waste considerably.

In addition to encouraging waste reduction, local governments help solve the solid waste problem in three other ways. They support recycling. They help collect trash and garbage. And they provide sanitary landfills or incinerators so that wastes that cannot be recycled are safely buried or burned. Public participation is most important for recycling and waste collection.

Recycling

Recycling wastes means using them as a resource to make new products. Thus, waste paper can be recycled to make new paper and old glass bottles can be recycled to make new bottles. In order to recycle materials, they must be separated—the paper from the glass, for example. Some recycling can be done at home. For instance, grass clippings and leaves can be turned into **compost** or **mulch**. One problem is that most people are not used to sorting their trash or to reusing it at home, but that is changing.

Local governments encourage recycling by urging people to separate materials that can be recycled and by telling people how they can reuse materials. They also support recycling by collecting recyclable materials.

Most of the manufacturing of new products from discarded materials is done by private industry. Paper companies use wastepaper to make new paper. Glass companies use discarded bottles to make new bottles. Local governments that collect these recyclables sell them to the manufacturing companies. The money the governments receive helps pay the cost of collecting the materials. Some cities and counties are also actually making recycled products themselves. Several cities and counties have begun to use yard wastes (grass clippings, leaves, even chipped wood) to make compost or mulch.

Local governments also support recycling by buying products made of recycled materials. By using recycled paper, for example, the governments create a greater demand for the old newspapers they want to sell for recycling.

Governments support recycling to protect natural resources. If old paper is reused, for example, fewer trees will need to be cut

Compost— decayed material which is used as fertilizer.

Mulch— material put around plants to prevent the growth of weeds and keep the soil from drying out.

Each year the Fayetteville Sanitation Division collects more than 12,000 tons of leaves, tree limbs, and other yard waste.

down to make new paper. Government officials also have a more direct interest in recycling: saving money. Burying trash in a sanitary landfill is very expensive. Burning solid wastes safely is even more expensive. Recycling can be an excellent way to save money because it reduces the amount of material going into the landfill. In 1989 the North Carolina General Assembly added another reason for interest in recycling. The General Assembly required that by 1993 local governments that operate landfills reduce by at least twenty-five percent the amount of waste that goes into the landfill.

Solid Waste Collection

Most cities and towns provide for house-to-house collection of solid waste. Once or twice a week, the "garbage truck" comes down each street and the crew empties the trash from the cans outside each house. (Usually, these are city crews and trucks. In some municipalities, however, the city hires private companies to collect solid wastes.) The truck—called a "packer"—is specially designed to crush the waste and press it together tightly so that it takes up as little space as possible.

Recycling collections are usually made on another day and with another kind of truck. The recycling truck has bins for different sorts of material. As the recycling crew empties the containers of recyclables left outside each house, they keep different kinds of materials separate. Not all municipalities have door-to-door recycling collections, however. In these towns, recycling centers provide bins in which people can deposit recyclable materials.

Catawba County was one of the first counties in the nation to provide house-to-house collection of recyclable materials. Most counties do not provide house-to-house solid-waste collection. Instead, residents of unincorporated areas either hire a private company to collect their trash or they take it to a waste collection site themselves. Bins to collect recyclable materials are often placed at waste collection sites. Most counties operate several waste collection sites. Sometimes the waste collection site consists of a large (usually green) box into which people put their trash. The box is emptied regularly into a very large packer truck. But if the box is not emptied often enough, or if people are not careful how they handle their trash, waste can spill out of the box. "Green box" sites can become very smelly, trash-covered places and create health hazards.

An alternative is the supervised waste collection site. Supervised sites have a packer right on the site. The packer operator sees that people put their trash into the packer, which immediately crushes the trash. Both the supervision and the immediate packing of the

Boxes and instructions for recycling are delivered to houses in the Town of Liberty.

waste helps prevent the mess and the hazard of "green box" sites.

Public cooperation is important whether the waste collection site is supervised or not. Wherever there is no house-to-house collection, people have more responsibility for safe collection of wastes and for recycling.

Some dangerous materials require special handling. State and federal regulations prohibit radioactive wastes and hazardous chemicals from being mixed with other solid wastes. These materials (including motor oil, paints and other household chemicals, tires, and automobile batteries) must be kept separate and cannot be collected through the regular collection system. You, your family, and other people in the community are responsible for sorting out these materials and making sure that they are collected appropriately.

Solid Waste Disposal

Once solid waste has been collected, local governments must dispose of it. Wastes can be recycled, burned, or buried. Each of these disposal methods requires special equipment and techniques to assure public safety. In North Carolina, each county is responsible for making sure solid wastes produced in the county are disposed of safely. Most counties operate their own landfills. Some counties hire private businesses or contract with cities to dispose of their solid wastes.

You have already learned about the recycling of materials that are separated at the source. Newspaper, for example, cannot be mixed with garbage or other wastes if it is to be used for making new paper. Yard wastes need to be kept free of glass and metal if they are to be used for making compost. However, some recycling can occur from wastes that have been mixed together. In a materials recovery operation, people sort through the solid wastes that have been collected, picking out such things as glass and cardboard. After that the remaining wastes can be passed through magnets to remove iron, and a special process removes aluminum. Materials recovery from mixed waste is only done rarely because it is very expensive. Separation at the source is much less expensive and much more frequently done, but it requires active public support to be effective.

Incineration—the safe burning of wastes.

The safe burning of wastes is also quite expensive. This process is called **incineration** and requires very special equipment. First, materials that will not burn (glass, metal, and rock, for example) must be sorted out. Then the burnable materials must be shredded. Special furnaces are required to burn the wastes at very high temperatures so that as many harmful chemicals as possible are destroyed by the fire. There is some smoke, however, even from a very hot, clean-burning fire. This smoke must be filtered and treated carefully to prevent air pollution.

How expensive are facilities for materials recovery and incineration? In 1992 a materials recovery and incineration plant being built for Bladen, Cumberland, and Hoke counties, cost over $50 million. To offset some of the cost of incineration, the heat from the fire will generate electricity and steam for a nearby factory. Nevertheless, incineration is not widely used because of the cost of the equipment and the complicated processes involved in making it safe.

Leachate—water that picks up impurities as it seeps through buried material,

The most common way to dispose of solid waste is to bury it. Safe burial of wastes requires the construction and the operation of a sanitary landfill. Sanitary landfills are quite different from the open dumps of the past. State and federal regulations now require that solid wastes be buried only in a properly constructed landfill. Special care must be taken to assure that the landfill does not pollute surface water or ground water. The landfill pit must be lined with plastic so that rainwater will not carry chemicals from the waste into the ground water. Any liquids or gases that do escape from a landfill must be captured and treated before being released.

Macon to open state-of-the-art landfill

Macon County Engineer Scott Wood is surrounded by rolls of plastic that will line a six-acre cell in Macon County's new landfill. The liner will help keep harmful chemicals from leaking out of the landfill and into the ground water.

by Bob Scott

Macon County contributes some 25,000 tons of garbage a year to the estimated 120 million tons dumped in the nearly 5,500 solid-waste landfills located throughout the U.S.

Macon County's landfill stands out from the others because it will be among the latest to use high-tech trash dumping technology.

If everything remains on schedule, on January 1 Macon County will begin using its $1.8-million landfill that will be the first in North Carolina to treat **leachate** (water that seeps through garbage and trash, and which can contaminate ground water) and will be the third in the state to use a synthetic liner to meet the new Environmental Protection Agency standards to cut the risk of groundwater contamination.

As counties run out of landfill space, they will have to construct landfills like Macon's to meet state and federal regulations, Macon County engineer Scott Wood said Wednesday.

Land costs are not cheap either. Macon County paid $1.2 million for 200 acres for its landfill.

The landfill has a design life of 30 years, Wood said.

The new landfill is being constructed in cells. The first 6-acre, 50-foot-deep cell will have 18 inches of compacted clay as a natural liner and another layer of high density synthetic liner on top of the clay. The first cell is expected to last the county six years.

The leachate will be piped to a pre-treatment facility where it will be treated and then piped through the Franklin water treatment plant, Wood said.

"It's changed a lot," said Horace Ledford, the county's solid waste supervisor.

"When I started 14 years ago, nearly anything could be dumped and we had only one front end loader to bury it. Now we have pans, front-end loaders, dozers, and compactors," Ledford said.

"The other big thing I've seen change is recycling. People are much more conscious of it," Ledford said.

— adapted from
Asheville Citizen-Times
Friday, September 20, 1991

Each day's waste must be covered with soil so that animals that might spread diseases are not attracted to the site. No fires are allowed. When the landfill is finally full, it must be covered more deeply with soil, planted with grass or trees, and monitored to make sure that any leaking liquids or gases are properly treated. Landfill operators direct the unloading of waste and see that it is properly covered. They must be specially trained to ensure safe handling of the wastes.

The costs of the land, of constructing the landfill, and of operating it according to state and federal regulations are considerable. To help pay these costs, many counties charge users "tipping fees" for all the waste they unload in the landfill. Some cities and counties charge individual households or businesses for the costs of collecting and disposing of their solid waste. The more waste they produce, the more they pay. Other local governments finance solid waste collection and disposal with taxes. The public can help keep these costs as low as possible by cutting down on what they throw away, by sorting out recyclable materials from the rest of the trash, and by buying products made from recycled materials.

PARKS AND RECREATION

Many local governments provide recreational opportunities for their residents. They build and maintain parks, which may have picnic tables, swing sets, ball fields, basketball and tennis courts, swimming pools, or other facilities. They operate recreation programs, which may include organized sports leagues, supervised swimming, instruction in crafts or games, and physical fitness programs. Parks provide safe, attractive places for people to enjoy themselves and to relax. Recreation programs extend opportunities for healthful exercise and relaxation.

Parks and recreation programs are staffed by people with many different specialties. A supervised swimming program, for example, requires a staff of qualified lifeguards. Not only must they know lifesaving techniques, but they must also know how to operate the pool's filtering system and how and when to add chemicals to keep the water safe for swimming. They also need to know how to communicate well with pool users to assure safe use of the pool.

Similarly, the recreation assistants who referee games, teach sports, or lead crafts sessions need to know not only the rules and techniques specific to that activity but also ways to communicate effectively and to treat everyone fairly. Park maintenance workers use a range of skills to keep parks safe and clean. Park and recreation directors need to know about all of these operations and to

Fayetteville park ranger Ron Harwood checks an owl recovering from an injury. Park rangers interpret nature and history to people who use the parks.

plan and coordinate them. Many directors have studied recreation administration in college.

Buying the land for a park, landscaping it, and building park facilities is a major investment for local government. Each park needs to be designed and built for heavy public use. After all, a park is a success only if people use it. But heavy use creates much wear and tear. Thus, parks also require constant maintenance. Equipment wears out and must be repaired or replaced. Keeping a park clean and in good repair costs money. Vandalism—the purposeful destruction of property—creates an even greater need for maintenance. Often a city or county does not have enough money to repair or replace park equipment that is broken before it would normally wear out.

People contribute to the success of a park by using it and by using it in ways that do not destroy the facilities or others' use and enjoyment of the park. Public cooperation is thus an essential part of every park and recreation program.

POLICE PROTECTION

Local law enforcement officers are available to help every North Carolina resident. Except for some of the smallest towns, each municipality in the state has its own police department. Gaston County and Mecklenburg County also have police departments. In the other 98 counties, sheriff's deputies provide police protection in unincorporated areas of the county and in towns without their own police department. Police officers and sheriff's deputies have similar duties and authority. In this section we will often refer to them together as "police."

To carry out their work, police must have special training. They study both criminal law (which defines illegal behavior) and constitutional law (which defines your rights, including your rights if you are suspected of a crime). They learn how and when to use weapons and other self-defense measures. They learn how to gather information and evidence.

Police officers also study ways to communicate clearly and to understand, respect, and deal with the differences among people. In fact, communicating with people and responding to their concerns for safety are today recognized as essential parts of police work. Most police realize that they need the respect and trust of the public. The people and the police must work together to produce safe communities.

Police help protect you and your community in three ways. They investigate crimes, they provide other emergency assistance, and they conduct patrol and other crime prevention operations.

Criminal Investigation

Although crimes are defined by the state legislature, most of the criminal investigation and crime prevention work in North Carolina is done by local police departments and sheriff's departments. Most criminal investigations begin when the victim or a witness calls the police. In many cities and counties, a special emergency telephone number, 911, reaches police and sheriff's departments. (Fire departments and emergency rescue squads can generally be reached through the 911 number as well.) Trained telephone operators ask the caller to describe the problem and the location of the victim.

If the crime is in progress, if the victim is injured, if the crime is very serious, or if a suspect is still on the scene, the **dispatcher** will radio police to respond immediately. The caller will usually be asked to stay on the line to inform responding officers about changes in the situation and help direct them to the location.

One or more officers might be dispatched, depending on the urgency and seriousness of the situation. Responding officers will stop any additional injury from happening and will make sure that emergency medical services are provided. The police will also arrest any suspects on the scene, interview the victim and witnesses about what happened, and inspect the scene. The officer in charge will then prepare an **incident report**, describing the crime and any suspects.

Dispatcher—
a person who gives emergency workers information so that those workers can respond to emergencies.

Incident report—
a report that a police officer writes describing a crime or other problem situation.

Computers help dispatchers locate the officer nearest to a caller who needs help. This system automatically shows the dispatcher the telephone number and address of the phone the caller is using.

If the crime has already occurred, the caller might be asked to wait for police to arrive, to make an appointment to meet with police at a more convenient time, or to give a report about the crime over the phone. Often only a single officer is dispatched to interview the victim or witness to a crime that has already occurred.

After the responding officer interviews victims and witnesses and inspects the scene, he or she will write an incident report describing the crime and any suspects. Responding officers turn in their incident reports before they leave work each day. Their supervisors review these reports and decide which crimes should be investigated further. The most serious crimes are usually assigned to detectives who specialize in criminal investigation. The officer who wrote the report or other officers who were assigned to patrol the area where the crime occurred might also be asked to investigate further.

Criminal investigations seek to identify the person(s) suspected of the crime, to gather evidence that can be used in court to convict the suspect, to arrest the suspect, and to recover any stolen property. Public cooperation is essential to effective criminal investigations. In the first place, police rely on victims and witnesses to

an interview with
Carolyn Hutchison
Captain
Police Department
Town of Carrboro, NC

As a rookie patrol officer, I worked undercover to help break a drug ring. I quickly saw how much some people are willing to hurt others, just to make lots of money. Later, as our department's juvenile officer, I saw cases of child abuse that made my heart sick. Protecting people from selfishly cruel criminals is a key part of police work. Helping to provide police protection gives me a great sense of accomplishment.

In my work in the police department, I have really been a "jack of all trades." As a patrol officer, I handled all kinds of complaints and requests for help from people in distress. As a detective, I investigated burglaries, rapes, murders, and other major crimes. As the department's crime prevention officer, I worked with residents and business managers to make their homes and businesses as safe from crime as possible. As juvenile officer, I investigated cases of child abuse and neglect and also worked with young people who had broken the law. Arresting a young boy or girl may seem harsh, but it is really a kindness when it helps them get back on the right path.

As a patrol sergeant, I supervised patrol officers during one of our twelve-hour shifts. You know that police are on patrol around the clock. That means that we have officers coming on duty at 6 a.m. and 6 p.m. to replace those who are going off-duty. As sergeant, my job was to direct officers about where to patrol, to review their work and the reports they wrote about each incident they dealt with, and to see that officers

in my patrol unit understood department policy and performed at their best as Carrboro police.

I am a small woman. Many people expect police officers to be men, often big men. Thus, I sometimes get startled looks or even comments like "You're awfully small . . ." Some people are surprised when I use my authority and skills to quiet an angry crowd or catch a fleeing criminal who is twice my weight. But I do it. My training and fitness have given me the knowledge, skill, and confidence I need to succeed as a police officer.

Now my job is more administrative. I supervise our detectives. That means I assign cases to the detectives, help them decide which are most in need of attention, and review their work with them. I also supervise DARE officers, our animal control officer, and administrative staff. Like other police departments, we report to the state and to the Federal Bureau of Investigation the number of crimes we learn about. I am responsible for our crime statistics and reporting. I also handle the department budget and coordinate our officers' in-service training.

Another important part of my work as captain is providing the public with information about the department. I issue press releases or meet with the press when we need to inform the public about how we are handling a case or how we need their help. I meet with people who want information about the department and our policies.

Police work is not just law enforcement. Our

Captain Carolyn Hutchison (left) discusses Carrboro's drug prevention programs with DARE officer, Darryl Roseboro.

department has a very clear service orientation. Only about ten to twenty percent of our activity is law enforcement. The rest is service: crime prevention, helping people who are locked out of cars or in need of other kinds of assistance, animal control, drug education in the schools, security at sports events, and traffic control, to name but a few. This is a career with many rewards. Helping the public is very satisfying work.

— interviewed by
Eric C. Peterson

Winston-Salem police officers interview a burglary victim.

report crimes. Unless people are willing to tell police about incidents that appear to involve a crime, most crimes will never come to police attention. Moreover, most suspects are identified from witness accounts. Much of the work of criminal investigation is interviewing victims and witnesses to obtain as full and complete an account of the incident as possible. People must be willing and able to tell police what they saw if police investigations are to be successful.

Other Emergency Assistance

Police also respond to other emergencies—everything from crowd control to traffic hazards, from missing persons to noisy parties. Many times people call these problems to police attention by phone, and officers are dispatched by radio. Other times, police see problems and intervene directly. For example, unsafe drivers are often stopped by police who observe their hazardous driving. Municipal police also investigate traffic accidents, although sheriff's deputies typically do not. Traffic accidents on rural roads and highways in North Carolina are investigated by the State Highway Patrol.

As with criminal investigations, public requests for service initiate most of the other emergency assistance police provide, and public cooperation with police is often needed for police assistance to be effective.

Crime Prevention

A large number of police activities are intended to help prevent crime. Police patrols (usually by car; sometimes on foot, bike, or horse) help discourage crime by making police visible throughout the community. Police sometimes concentrate their patrols in areas where there have been frequent reports of crime. In addition to patrol, police attempt to prevent crime by informing people about ways to protect their property and themselves. Police also help people learn nonviolent ways to solve arguments and find ways to avoid getting involved in criminal activities. After all, police cannot be everywhere at once. Crime prevention depends on the entire community.

WHO BENEFITS FROM PUBLIC SERVICES?

As you have seen, user-focused public services have both individual and community-wide benefits. If only the customer benefits, private business can provide the service. People will buy a service because they want it. No public money or authority is needed. Local governments provide services when public officials decide there are important community-wide benefits. These include the benefits of seeing that everyone has access to essential services, as well as improvements for the community as a whole.

5 Improving the Community

Making the community a better place to live is a major goal of local governments. In one way, of course, all public services help improve the community. As you learned in Chapter Four, user-focused services (like waste disposal and criminal investigation) help not only the people who use the service directly, but also their neighbors and even people who only work, shop, or travel through the community. Most public services help both people who use them directly and the community at large.

This chapter focuses on services that have no direct users. These services are specifically intended to help make the entire community better. Planting flowers in public areas, encouraging **economic development**, and improving human relations are examples of these "community-focused" services. They are intended to change the physical, economic, or social setting in which people live and work. These services are designed for the benefit of an entire neighborhood or other community. This chapter discusses programs that improve physical conditions, economic conditions, and social conditions in the community.

Governments can support community improvement in three ways: by delivering public service, by encouraging private action, and by regulating private behavior. Take the problem of litter as an example. Litter is trash that is thrown out along streets or roads or in other public places. In the public service approach to litter control,

Economic development—
activities to create new jobs and additional sales and other business.

Well-maintained parks beautify many North Carolina communities. Here a city worker cares for the grounds in Fayetteville.

a government hires someone to pick up the litter. One alternative is for government to encourage people to pick up litter. (For example, the North Carolina Department of Transportation's "Adopt a Highway" program encourages community organizations and businesses to pick up trash voluntarily along rural roads all across the state.) Or governments can try to control litter through regulation—making littering illegal and imposing fines on people who are convicted of littering. This chapter focuses on public service and encouragement approaches to community betterment. Chapter 6 addresses regulation of private behavior.

THE COMMUNITY'S PHYSICAL CONDITION

Local governments often seek to change or protect the physical condition of their communities. To do this, local governments establish programs to protect people and property from natural hazards and pests, as well as programs to make their communities more attractive places to live and work.

In many places, local governments build and maintain drainage ditches or levees to help prevent flooding. Coastal towns have programs to replenish the sand on eroded beaches. Cities in the piedmont and mountains have programs to remove snow and ice from their streets. These services are typically carried out by the local government's public works department.

Counties throughout the state have programs to control mosquitoes, rats, stray dogs, and other potentially harmful animals. The county health department sprays for mosquitoes and poisons rats. Many local governments also have an animal control office. However, voluntary animal protection societies also contract with local governments to operate shelters for dogs and other stray animals and to encourage responsible pet ownership.

City crews, like these in Burlington, remove snow from streets and spread sand so traffic can move safely.

Historic preservation programs identify and protect buildings and areas that have special significance in a community. These programs encourage pride in the community and its heritage and help to keep old buildings and neighborhoods from becoming run-down (or to fix up those that are run-down). Local governments support historic preservation in several ways. Many governments have sponsored building inventories to identify and describe

The Old Salem historic district is one of many in the state that preserves buildings from the past. Attractive neighborhoods like these are pleasant places to live. Historic districts also attract tourists and, thus, help create jobs in many North Carolina communities.

buildings of historic or architectural interest. Publication of the inventory may encourage the owners of the listed buildings to maintain those buildings in good condition or even to restore them to their original appearance.

Local governments can also provide incentives for maintaining and restoring historic buildings, such as making low-interest loans available. Banks or other local companies may also join with local government in support of historic preservation or other efforts to prevent the deterioration or to encourage the restoration of neighborhoods.

Sometimes, buildings are in such poor condition that they are beyond repair and unsafe to use. Local governments can buy these buildings and demolish them to remove the hazard.

Government beautification programs include planting trees and flowers, and installing public art displays, flags, and holiday decorations. Litter control may involve providing convenient trash baskets or litter pickup. Efforts like these are often paid for by counties or municipalities and carried out by government employees. Sometimes, however, the government might hire a private company to do the work or assign the work to people who have been convicted of driving while intoxicated or other offenses.

Local governments also encourage garden clubs or civic organizations to do community beautification and litter control. The general public can be encouraged to help, too. Campaigns publicize the benefits of an attractive community and urge people to "pick up, paint up, fix up." Contests to see who can pick up the most litter or produce the most beautiful flower beds provide a way to recognize outstanding efforts. Often, much of the work to improve the physical condition of a community is done by **volunteers**—people who give their time and effort to making their neighborhoods safer and more attractive.

THE COMMUNITY'S ECONOMIC CONDITION

Local governments are interested in attracting and keeping businesses in their communities because businesses provide jobs and pay taxes. The people in a community need jobs to earn incomes. Taxes paid by businesses can help reduce the taxes residents have to pay to support local government. For these reasons, many local governments seek to play an important part in shaping the community's economy.

In North Carolina, more than 60 counties have formed economic development commissions to improve their local economies. Many cities also support economic development, often by helping fund the local **chamber of commerce**. Economic development commissions attract new industries and other businesses and support existing business and industries. The commissions collect information about the local economy and work force, advertise the advantages of their communities, and help businesses organize support that they may need from local government and others. For example, the economic development commission may work with businesses, local schools, and community colleges to help the schools and colleges develop job training needed by the businesses. Or the economic development commission may work

Volunteers—
people who donate their time and effort.

Chamber of commerce—
a group of business people formed to promote business interests in the community.

Stereotype—
a set of untested beliefs about the members of a group.

Infrastructure—
basic public services such as water, sewers, and roads that are needed for economic development.

an interview with
Ted Abernathy
Orange County Economic Development
Director

The profession of economic development has changed so much over the past 20 years that the **stereotype** of a used-car salesman-type trying to push any and all business on a particular community is no longer close to the truth.

Business retention, small business technical assistance, visitor services, affordable housing, technology transfer, and employee training are now key components of most economic development programs.

The Orange County Economic Development Strategic Plan, adopted in 1989, establishes the local mission as "ensuring the desired quality of life in Orange County by encouraging economic development through investment in human resources, the expansion of existing businesses, and the creation of diversified and environmentally safe businesses. The aim of this investment is to provide jobs for county residents and to increase the nonresidential tax base, thus enhancing the quality of life."

Our local plan calls for activities in small-business planning, **infrastructure**, tourism, education, planning, and job training. To gain the information necessary to be effective in such diverse areas, our staff is involved in many organizations and we serve on many boards. Some, such as the local Chambers of Commerce, Downtown Commission, and Raleigh-Durham Regional Association, might be expected. Others may be surprising.

I serve as chairman of the Advisory Committee to the Orange County JOBS Program. The program is operated by the Department of Social Services and is aimed at welfare families. The objective is to help people on public assistance gain economic self-sufficiency. My economic development concerns are the development of a broadened employee pool. Orange County's unemployment rate was the lowest of all the counties in North Carolina last year. Labor supply is a business issue.

The Triangle J Council of Governments has appointed a group to work on recycling plastics. Solid waste disposal and environmental issues are a growing concern. Our group works on all components of the process: collection, identifying and recruiting manufacturers, and developing users for recycled products.

Transportation, land-use planning, recreation, and public health all play integral parts in the quality of economic development in our community. When economic development professionals recruit a new company or help a local business expand, our job doesn't end. The goal is to maintain and improve our quality of life. New, retained, or expanded businesses can bring jobs and taxes. They can reduce the burden on the residential taxpayer. They can provide those in need the means to meet their needs.

But they can also create traffic, noise, and demands on local services. They can create competition that results in closed businesses, lost jobs, and vacant buildings. Economic development is not an instant solution to all a community's problems nor is it the devil in disguise. Done properly, it is a set of programs and tools that helps a community reach its goals.

— adapted from
Chapel Hill Newspaper
October 13, 1991

with a **business development corporation** to create an industrial park or to renew a downtown area.

In Kinston, a business development group called the Committee of 100 worked with the Lenoir County Development Commission, Lenoir County, and the City of Kinston to develop an industrial park at the edge of the city. With a $3.5 million grant from the State of North Carolina, the city expanded its water, sewer, and electric services so that it could serve new industries that might locate in the industrial park. (Kinston is one of 72 cities in North Carolina which operates a municipal electric company.) As a result of these efforts, a large dishwasher factory and several other industrial plants chose to locate in Kinston. Overall, more than 3,000 new jobs were added in manufacturing. Additional jobs were added because stores and other businesses needed more employees to serve the people working in the new factories.

Sometimes, local governments work directly with a business development corporation. For example, in Fayetteville, city and county governments worked with a business development corporation called Fayetteville Progress to improve the city's downtown.

Busses bring people into downtown Fayetteville. New store fronts, trees, streetlights, and paving make this an attractive place to work and shop.

Fayetteville Progress was formed by local business leaders to organize the downtown renewal. Fayetteville Progress coordinated the efforts of the City of Fayetteville and Cumberland County and various banks and real estate developers to clear out some old buildings, to remodel others, and to build new offices, stores, and apartments. Asheville, New Bern, Raleigh, Wilmington, and many other cities and towns have also worked with business development corporations to improve their downtowns.

Preparing property for development by installing water lines, sewers, and roads; constructing buildings; offering low-interest loans; coordinating job training with schools and community colleges—all these are special efforts to make the community more attractive to business and industry.

Because tourism is a major part of the economy in many parts of North Carolina, some cities and counties devote considerable efforts toward making their communities more attractive to tourists. Tourism is especially important to the economy of the mountains, the coast, and the sandhills in the south central piedmont. In addition, all of the largest cities in the state actively seek to host conventions, adding another aspect to the tourism industry.

Cary's Lazy Daze Arts and Crafts Fair attracts thousands of people to Cary each year.

The 25 cities that belong to the North Carolina Association of Conventions and Visitors Bureaus spend more than $12 million each year to attract paying visitors to their communities. Together, these cities employ more than 150 people in their tourism bureaus. Many other towns and cities also have programs to attract tourists.

Special efforts to promote tourism include festivals like Spivey's Corners' "Hollerin' Contest" and outdoor dramas like Boone's "Horn in the West." Advertising is important, too. Brochures and maps identify interesting places and events to entice visitors. Coliseums, stadiums, museums, and arts centers also help to attract tourists. Cities and counties support these places, in part at least for the tourist business they generate.

Historic sites are major tourist attractions throughout North Carolina. One benefit of historic preservation programs is that they help develop and maintain areas of historic interest to tourists. Similarly, community beautification, recreation, and arts programs that local governments support for the benefit of their own residents frequently help attract tourists, too.

These same features may also help attract new businesses and industries. In addition, an abundant supply of safe water, adequate sewage-disposal capacity, good police and fire protection, good schools, and other public services that support a high quality of life are important to business and industry leaders who are looking for new locations for facilities. Thus, good "user-focused" services also contribute to economic development.

SOCIAL RELATIONSHIPS IN THE COMMUNITY

Local governments also work to improve social relations in their communities. Some local governments have county-wide or city-wide programs to promote understanding among different racial, ethnic, or religious groups and to encourage fair treatment of all people in the community. These efforts may be organized through a human relations commission. Another approach concentrates on improving relations among people in a particular neighborhood. Local governments support these efforts through community action agencies, through neighborhood or residents' associations, or even through police community-relations offices.

In North Carolina most human relations commissions were established to improve race relations. Even today relationships among North Carolinians of African, European, and Native American descent too often continue conflicts that began centuries ago. European settlers fought with Native Americans (whom the English colonists called "Indians") for control of the land. Soon some Europeans began to bring captive Africans here as slaves.

Myths about differences between the races and attitudes about European superiority that began during the Indian wars and during slavery continue to be learned and believed by many people. After the Civil War, slavery was abolished and the former slaves became full citizens. Black North Carolinians participated actively in politics and were elected to state and local public offices, as well as to Congress. However, many whites in North Carolina continued to fear and look down on the former slaves (and on the few Native Americans still living in the state). In the late nineteenth century, a white majority in the General Assembly passed laws requiring segregation of the races. These minorities were denied basic civil rights, and government officials even overlooked violence against them. By 1900, few of North Carolina's African American or Native American citizens were able to vote or hold public office.

Not until the 1960s did many African American and Native American North Carolinians regain their basic civil rights including the right to vote. Federal voting-rights laws ended **poll taxes** and other practices used to keep people from voting. Only then was segregation ended. Many white North Carolinians supported ending segregation and assuring civil rights for all North Carolinians. However, some whites continued to fear African Americans and Native Americans and to feel superior to them. At the same time, some African Americans and Native Americans continued to resent whites because of a long history of discrimination and mistreatment.

Poll tax—

a tax people had to pay in order to be able to vote.

Human relations commissions were established primarily to find ways to ease racial tensions and to eliminate racial discrimination. The commissions hold public meetings to discuss potential problems among racial groups. Much of their work is getting people of different races to talk and listen to one another. The commissions try to help people realize that cultural differences do not need to be threatening and to help them see the individuality of people whose race is different from their own. Getting beyond the racial stereotype to see the individual person is an important step in eliminating racism.

Human relations commissions also deal with other problems of intolerance and discrimination based on race, ethnic group, religion, or gender. In recent years, new immigrants have come to North Carolina from Latin America and from Asia. Sometimes they are the subject of discrimination or abuse by others who fear or resent them because of their race or origin.

Also, there is a growing variety of religious affiliations in North Carolina. Protestants remain the largest group, but there are also Catholics and people of other Christian denominations, Jews, Muslims, Buddhists, and people of many other religions now living in the state. Human relations commissions try to help promote understanding of other religions and to prevent acts of religious discrimination.

A somewhat different social problem concerns relationships between women and men. Many deeply held attitudes about the roles of men and women developed when almost all women were married and worked full time at home. In recent years these social patterns have changed. Now most women work outside the home. Many women are single heads of households. Laws and social

In neighborhoods across North Carolina, citizens groups have organized to keep their communities drug free.

expectations about how men should treat women are changing. Married women now have the same property rights as their husbands, for example. Domestic violence is no longer treated as a "family" matter, but is now the crime of assault—a matter for the police and the courts to deal with. Human relations commissions help set up ways for men and women who are concerned about these changes to communicate with each other in order to understand each other better.

Local governments may also work with residents of a neighborhood to build trust and a sense of responsibility for one another. Crime and other social problems are often greatest in areas where people do not trust their neighbors or do not believe that they can or should do anything for each other. Community Action Programs and other neighborhood-based programs help people work together on projects to benefit the neighborhood. Residents' councils can promote cooperation and improvement in public housing or help youths fight drug abuse.

Police can also encourage neighborhood cooperation. For example, Greensboro police set up Police Neighborhood Resource Centers in the city's public housing communities. Each of these police mini-stations has two officers who are permanently assigned there. The officers patrol the housing communities on foot and get to know the residents. In addition to criminal investigations and emergency response services, these officers help residents get the social services and health services they need. Some services are even provided right in the mini-station. The officers also organize recreation for neighborhood youth. As a result of the police officers' efforts, people have begun to trust each other and the police, increasing residents' willingness to report crimes, ask for police assistance, and assist the police. This increased cooperation with police reduces crime and makes the neighborhood safer for all the residents.

DECIDING WHAT TO DO

People sometimes disagree about what local government should do to improve the community. One source of disagreement is differences about how much change is desirable. Some people might want more ditching or beach erosion-control devices, but others might want to limit human interference with natural drainage or beach movement. Another source of disagreement concerns the relative importance of various public programs. Some people place high value on an attractive community and want to see public funds spent on improving community appearance. Others may

Town's bid to attract business is challenged

By Kim Brooks
Staff writer

Some Garner shop owners are crying foul after the town secured a low-interest loan to help lure a new restaurant.

As part of its fledgling effort to attract new businesses, Garner applied for a $250,000 loan from the state's Community Development Block Grant program for Fitzgerald's restaurant.

"The state gives it to us, and we loan it to Fitzgerald's and they pay it back to us," said Rex Todd, Garner's economic development director. "The state is very selective, so I think this is quite an honor for this town."

But not everyone is happy with the deal.

Some business owners say the state-sponsored loan gives an unfair advantage to the competition and turns their own tax money against them.

"You're obligating tax dollars to help a business come in here and compete with businesses that are already here," said Ralph F. Sullivan, owner of the Archery Shop. "It's just not an equitable situation."

Merchants worry the town will be held accountable if the restaurant fails. And they wonder why the money was used for an out-of-town business rather than a local enterprise. Fitzgerald's has locations in Sanford and Southern Pines.

"My first reaction was that the town shouldn't be financing a retail business," said Gene Hornick, owner of Simply Scrumptious deli. "I'd feel a lot better if it was someone who's a part of the community. If someone's going to get a break, it should be someone who has contributed to our community."

Mr. Todd said local businesses could try for a loan as well, but like other companies, they must meet state criteria.

To qualify, a business must match the loan amount dollar-for-dollar. Also, 60 percent of the jobs created must go to low-to-moderate-income people. And the amount of the loan must fall within the state limit of $15,000 for each new job created.

Garner boosted its search for more businesses and industry to pump up its tax base by appointing Mr. Todd full-time economic development director. The town also created a committee to plot a recruiting strategy.

But two members of the board of aldermen questioned the town's role in the agreement.

The board split 3-2 in approving the loan pact, with aldermen Janice Stephenson, Michael Adams and Ronnie Williams supporting it. Aldermen H. Wayne Britt and Steve Grodensky voted against it.

"The main reason I voted against it was I don't feel the town should get into the financing business," Mr. Britt said.
—adapted from
The News and Observer
November 6, 1991

---

argue that public funds should be spent on public services that they consider more important. People might also differ about the kinds of new industry that government should encourage or even whether additional economic development is good for their community. People might also have different views about desirable social relations in the community.

Proposal—

a suggestion put forward for approval.

Proposals for public programs to improve the community are usually presented long before any action is taken. Often, an initial discussion at a meeting of the city council or board of county commissioners introduces a proposal to both elected officials and the public. Proposals may be developed by the city or county manager, by other staff members, by appointed advisory boards, by elected officials, or by private citizens.

News reporters play an important part in spreading word of a new proposal to the public. Stories in newspapers or on radio or television inform people in the community about the proposal. Groups of people with similar interests may also pay particular attention to the topics discussed by the governing board and alert their members when an issue of particular concern comes up. For example, the local real estate dealers' association and environmental protection groups like the Sierra Club might both be interested in a proposed change in drainage ditches, although for different reasons. The real estate agents might support the plan in order to protect buildings or to create more building sites. On the other hand, the environmental protection groups might oppose the plan because they fear it would harm wildlife or water quality.

People who favor or oppose a proposal can express their concerns about it in various ways. They may write letters to the editor or give interviews to news reporters. They may speak to friends and to members of groups with whom they share common interests. They may speak at public meetings or talk to the city or county manager or other staff members. Most importantly, however, they must communicate their concerns to members of the local government's governing board. The elected representatives on the governing board have the authority and the responsibility to decide whether or not to approve the proposal. People call or write their elected representatives and present **petitions** signed by many voters to express their opinions about a proposal. According to North Carolina's "Open Meetings Law," the governing board's meetings must be open to the public. Thus, reporters can cover the debates and publicize the arguments for and against proposed programs. **Proponents** and **opponents** can attend these meetings and express their opinions to elected officials.

Petition—
a request for government action signed by a number of voters.

Proponent—
a person or organization that supports a proposal.

Opponent—
a person or organization that is against a proposal.

Often, plans are changed to reflect the concerns of opponents while continuing to meet the most important objectives of the proponents. Sometimes, however, elected officials are unable or unwilling to adopt a program that pleases everyone. Opponents who feel strongly about the plan may continue to try to prevent it even after it has been adopted. They might file a lawsuit, asking the courts to stop work on the program. Or they might campaign against representatives who voted for the program, hoping to elect new members of the governing board who will vote to stop the program. Of course, those who supported the proposal are likely to continue their interest in it and to go on backing the members of the board who voted for the plan.

Once a program has been authorized by the governing board,

local government employees begin to carry it out. Many approaches to community improvement also require active public cooperation to succeed. The organized cooperation of businesses, community groups, schools, and other parts of the community is very important for many community improvement activities. Programs that are designed to encourage people to fix up their property, pick up litter, or work with their neighbors to improve community relations all depend on the people in a community for their success.

6 Regulating Harmful Behavior

One of the most powerful tools local governments have to improve their communities is the authority to regulate harmful behavior within their jurisdictions. North Carolina state law gives counties and municipalities authority to regulate various activities to protect people from harm. For example, local governments can pass "leash laws" requiring owners to control their dogs, reducing the danger of people being bitten. Local governments can adopt building restrictions to prevent people from constructing buildings in areas that are likely to be flooded. City governments set speed limits and other regulations for traffic on city streets.

Who decides what behavior is likely to be harmful enough to need regulation? How are those decisions made? What kinds of behavior do North Carolina cities and counties frequently regulate? How do they enforce those regulations? These are the questions this chapter answers.

Traffic laws help make streets safer by regulating how people drive. Police enforce traffic laws on city streets.

Crime—

an act that is forbidden by law. A crime is an offense against all of the people of the state, not just the victim of the act.

Governments regulate personal behavior that threatens people's ability to live and work together in safety and security. Many of the laws against disruptive behavior are made by the state General Assembly. For example, state laws declare certain acts to be **crimes**. Crimes are offenses against all of the people of North Carolina, not just the victim who is harmed directly by the act. State laws also provide rules for the safe operation of cars and trucks on the state's highways. State laws apply to the entire state.

Local governments also have the responsibility to determine what kind of public order they want to encourage within their jurisdictions. But there are limits to their authority to regulate. Local government regulations must not violate either the state or federal constitution, and local governments must have authority for their regulations from the state of North Carolina. Local governments in North Carolina have broad authority to regulate behavior that creates a public nuisance and threatens the public health, safety, or welfare. Other kinds of local regulation require special acts of authorization by the General Assembly.

In the News . . .

Editorial

Yard Wastes: Burning Ban Prudent

The custom of burning leaves and grass clippings, long considered a rural rite of passage, could be headed for extinction in Durham County. The county commissioners have asked the deputy county attorney to draft an ordinance that would ban open burning.

The commissioners have taken the right step to address this issue. Two main factors make this action timely and necessary. First, open burning could become a potential public health problem as the county grows and becomes more urban. What was once a legitimate way to dispose of yard waste will become a nuisance for others. Besides the smoke, open burning releases harmful gases such as carbon monoxide into the air, further adding to pollution caused by automobiles.

Second, the county is fast running out of places to put yard wastes. After January 1, state law requires that all counties stop disposing of yard wastes in landfills. With dumping of yard wastes thus prohibited, more residents are likely to resort to burning as a means of disposal.

The commissioners cannot wait for that deadline to pass before addressing this problem.

Even if the county approves a ban, the problem of what to do with yard wastes will remain. As they debate a ban on burning, the commissioners should also consider ways to help residents cope with the yard waste problem.

The county has several options it may consider. Residents could be encouraged to use their yard clippings to make mulch and compost. The county could also work with city sanitation officials to expand the yard waste recycling program at the Durham landfill. County officials also may have to consider some limited pickup service for yard wastes.

Some residents will frown upon the prospect of a burning ban, viewing it as an unnecessary government intrusion. But as Durham County grows, changes in old habits are inevitable— including the custom of watching yard wastes go up in smoke.
— adapted from
The Herald Sun
June 3, 1992

Behavior that is acceptable in one community may be regulated as a nuisance in another community. For example, while some local governments have ordinances that require dog owners to keep their dogs penned or on a leash, not all do so. Some cities and towns have ordinances regulating the loudness and/or the time of noisy behavior in residential areas. Some local governments prohibit burning trash or leaves. Views about the seriousness of the harm caused by an activity often vary from place to place across North Carolina.

Views about the harmfulness of an activity also change over time. For example, many cities and towns in North Carolina used to require stores to be closed all day on Sunday. Over the past 30 years, most of those ordinances have been repealed. In many parts of the state, more people wanted to shop on Sunday, and more merchants wanted to sell on Sunday. Fewer people believed it was wrong to conduct business on Sunday (or, even if they believed it was wrong, that the government should keep others from shopping on Sunday). Not everyone agreed, however. Often, as change occurs, some people continue to hold on to their old views of an activity, while others come to see its harmfulness quite differently. Controversy is likely to be great whenever people within a community have different views about how harmful an activity is. Thus, in a number of cities and towns there was considerable public debate over repeal of the ordinances requiring businesses to close on Sunday.

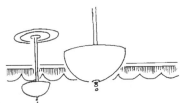

More recently, there has been considerable controversy as North Carolina communities have begun to regulate smoking in public places. In this case, the old view was that smoking was not a public problem. In fact, the use of tobacco was even seen by some North Carolinians as a sort of patriotic duty. Tobacco was North Carolina's chief crop. Much of the state's economy depended on raising tobacco, wholesaling it, and manufacturing cigarettes and other tobacco products. This traditional view began to be challenged as medical researchers linked tobacco smoke to cancer, heart disease, and breathing disorders. Evidence that nonsmokers' health can be injured by breathing secondhand smoke has increased the conviction among many people that smoking tobacco in public places should be prohibited. And as fewer and fewer people in the United States smoke, tobacco has also become a smaller part of the state's economy.

Local government regulation of smoking in public places is still a very controversial topic in North Carolina. The case of Greensboro provides a good illustration of how people participate in a local government's decision to regulate behavior. In June 1988, Greensboro resident Lori Faley presented the Greensboro City Council a petition asking the council to regulate smoking in public places. Ms. Faley started the petition after someone blew smoke in her face while she stood in a supermarket checkout lane. The petition she brought to the city council had more than 500 signatures and called for an ordinance regulating smoking in stores and restaurants, as well as in publicly owned buildings. There was immediate opposition to the ordinance, especially from tobacco companies and workers in Greensboro. (More than 2,300 people were employed in the tobacco industry there.) Some merchants were also opposed, fearing smoking regulations would be bad for their businesses, too. The city council held a public hearing on the request and then appointed a committee to study the issue.

The committee was to be made up of representatives from the city council, the county commission, the county health department, and business owners and managers. But it was slow to organize, and did not hold its first meeting until July 1989.

Ms. Faley and her group, which became known as GASP (Greensboro Against Smoking Pollution), were frustrated at the council's response and did not wait for the committee to meet. GASP took advantage of a provision in the Greensboro Charter for procedures called **initiative** and **referendum**. Initiative is a procedure by which voters submit a petition to propose an ordinance. Referendum is a procedure by which the voters themselves approve or reject an ordinance. (Greensboro is one of only a few North Carolina cities with provisions for initiative and referendum.)

The GASP petition called for the council to vote on the ordinance regulating smoking in public places. It also called for a referendum on the ordinance if the council failed to adopt it. The initiative petition required the valid signatures of 7,247 Greensboro voters to force a referendum.

In August 1989, GASP submitted its petition. Although more than 10,000 people had signed the petition, only 7,306 signatures were certified as those of registered Greensboro voters. However, that was more than the number necessary to require a vote. The council refused to adopt the ordinance, and the referendum was placed on the ballot for the November election.

Greensboro tobacco companies spent tens of thousands of dollars urging voters to defeat the ordinance. They printed brochures opposing the ordinance and mailed them to voters. They used other advertising. One company had employees at each of the city's 45 voting places to encourage voters to reject the ordinance.

Initiative—
a way in which citizens propose laws by gathering voter signatures on a petition. Only a few cities and no counties in North Carolina are authorized to use initiative.

Referendum—
an election in which citizens vote directly on a public policy question.

Fire Prevention and Protection, Sec. **10-6. Smoking prohibited in specified public places.**

(a) *Generally.* No person shall smoke or carry a lighted cigar, cigarette, pipe or match or use any spark, flame or fire-producing device in any of the following places:

(1) Elevators, regardless of capacity, for use by the general public.

(2) Public areas of museums, art galleries, public libraries, Greensboro Civic Cultural Center and Natural Science Center.

(3) Seating areas and adjacent aisles of theatres and the Greensboro Coliseum Arena.

(4) Retail stores designed and arranged to accommodate more than two hundred (200) persons, or in which twenty-five (25) persons are regularly employed. The prohibition of this subparagraph shall not apply to smoking rooms, restrooms, restaurants, executive offices or beauty parlors in retail stores when specifically approved by the fire inspector by written order to the person having control of the premises upon a finding that such use therein does not constitute a fire hazard.

(5) Duly designated nonsmoking area of a restaurant. For this purpose, the owner of every restaurant, whether currently in existence or to be established in the future, with an indoor seating capacity of fifty (50) or more seats shall designate a nonsmoking area consisting of at least twenty-five (25) percent of the indoor seating capacity of the restaurant. In areas where smoking is prohibited, existing physical barriers and ventilation systems shall be used to the greatest extent possible to minimize the smoke in adjacent nonsmoking areas. Provided, this subparagraph shall not apply to: Bars and cocktail lounges; nor shall the seating capacity of any bar or lounge located within a restaurant be included in the calculation of the total seating capacity of the restaurant nor rooms used for private functions or banquets.

(b) *Placarding required.* Every person having control of premises upon which smoking or the carrying of lighted objects is prohibited by or under the authority of this section shall conspicuously display upon the premises signs reading "Nonsmoking Area—Smoking Prohibited by Law." Such signs must be of standard size and lettering approved by the fire inspector.

(c) *Sign removal prohibited.* No person shall remove or deface any placard required to be erected by or under the authority of this section.

(d) *Civil penalty.* Any person violating subsection (a) during the first year from the effective date hereof (1 January 1990) shall be given a warning of violation only. Thereafter, any person who shall violate subsection (a) shall be subject to payment of a civil penalty of twenty-five dollars ($25.00). Any person, or his agent, having control of any premises or place who knowingly permits a violation of subsection (a) without requesting the violator to comply shall be subject to payment of the civil penalty provided for herein. Any duly authorized local government official is authorized to either send a civil penalty citation to the violator by certified mail or personally deliver such citation to the violator stating the nature of the violation, the amount of the penalty, and directing that the violator pay the penalty to the city tax collector's office within fourteen (14) days of receipt.

(e) *Misdemeanor and civil violation.* A violation of either subsection (b) or subsection (c) shall constitute a misdemeanor and shall also subject the person in violation to a payment of a civil penalty of twenty-five dollars ($25.00).

(Ord. No. 89-128, § 1, 9-28-89; Ord. No. 89-151, §§ 1–3, 11-16-89)

GASP did not have similar financial resources, but the group did have the names of those who had signed the petition. GASP members called those people to urge them to vote for the ordinance. The ordinance passed by a very narrow margin: 14,991 to 14,818.

That election did not end the controversy, however. Tobacco workers in Greensboro began an initiative petition of their own. This time the petition called for a referendum to repeal the smoking regulation ordinance that the voters adopted in 1989. The petitioners collected the required number of signatures, and another election was held in 1991. Voters rejected repealing the ordinance by more than two to one. Although thousands of people in Greensboro were still unhappy with the city's regulation of smoking in public places, Greensboro voters overwhelmingly supported keeping the ordinance.

REGULATING THE USE OF PROPERTY

Local governments regulate the use of property to protect the physical environment, to encourage economic development, or to protect people's health and safety. Several different kinds of property regulations are commonly used.

In many jurisdictions, a land-use plan serves as the basis for much of the regulation of property use. City or county planners (or outside consultants) study the physical characteristics of the land. (Where are the steep slopes? What areas are subject to flooding?) They map existing streets, rail lines, water lines, sewers, schools, parks, fire stations, and other facilities that can support development. They also note current uses of the land. (Where are the factories, the warehouses, the stores and offices, the residential neighborhoods?)

On the basis of their studies, the plan-

City planners use maps to help them regulate land use. Here Roy Walston of the City of Rocky Mount checks official maps.

ners prepare maps showing how various areas might be developed to make use of existing public facilities and to avoid mixing uses (keeping factories and junkyards separate from houses, for instance). The maps may also indicate where new water lines and sewers might be built most easily. These maps are then presented to the public for comment. After the public has reviewed the maps, the planners prepare a detailed set of maps showing current and possible future uses of the land. The local governing board may review and vote on this final set of maps itself or delegate planning authority to an appointed planning board. The approved maps become the official land-use plan.

All but the smallest North Carolina cities and towns have land-use plans. Municipal land-use plans typically cover an area one mile beyond the municipal boundaries. The area outside the city limits, but under the city's planning authority, is called the **extraterritorial land-use planning jurisdiction**. With the approval of the county commissioners, a city may extend its extraterritorial land-use planning jurisdiction even farther.

Counties have authority to regulate land use only over the parts of the county not subject to city planning. Because of cities' extraterritorial jurisdiction for land-use planning, the county land-use planning area is even smaller than the unincorporated area of the county. By 1992, a total of 89 North Carolina counties had adopted land-use plans.

Local government officials can use land-use plans to guide their decisions about where to locate new public facilities. Some governments use them only for these nonregulatory purposes. A land-use plan also establishes a basis for regulation of property uses. However, the plan itself does not set up a system of regulation. **Zoning** and **subdivision regulation** are systems of regulation based on a land-use plan.

Zoning

Zoning sets up restrictions on the use of land. The local governing board establishes categories of land use. Then the categories are applied to specific areas of the jurisdiction, creating zones for different kinds of development. The categories specify the kinds of activities the land can and cannot be used for and various requirements for developing and using the land. For example, one residential category might be for single-family houses. That category might prohibit any apartments or commercial or industrial activity in the zone. It might also require that each lot be a minimum size and that buildings be constructed a specified distance from the boundaries of the lot. Another zoning category might be commer-

Extraterritorial land-use planning jurisdiction—
the area outside city limits over which a city has authority for planning and regulating land use.

Zoning—
rules designating different areas of land for different uses. For instance, some land might be zoned for houses, other land for stores, and still other land for factories.

Subdivision regulation—
rules for dividing land for development.

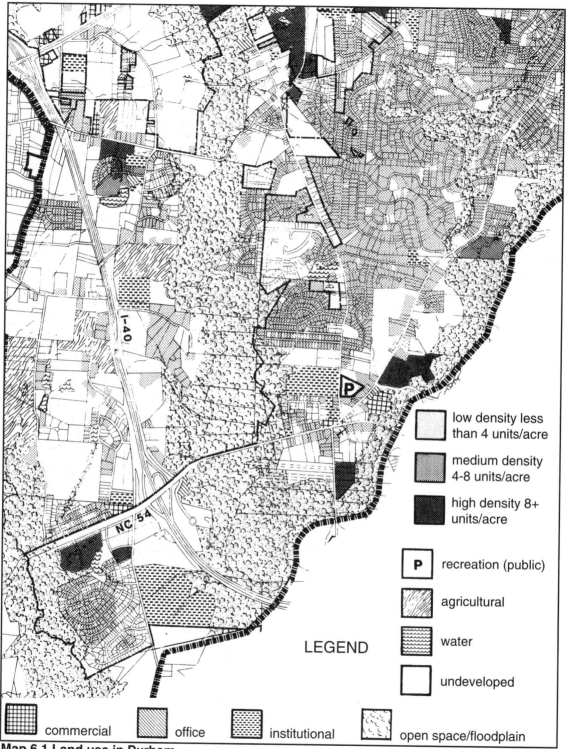

Map 6.1 Land use in Durham.

LEGEND

low density less than 4 units/acre	
medium density 4-8 units/acre	
high density 8+ units/acre	
P recreation (public)	
agricultural	
water	
undeveloped	

commercial   office   institutional   open space/floodplain

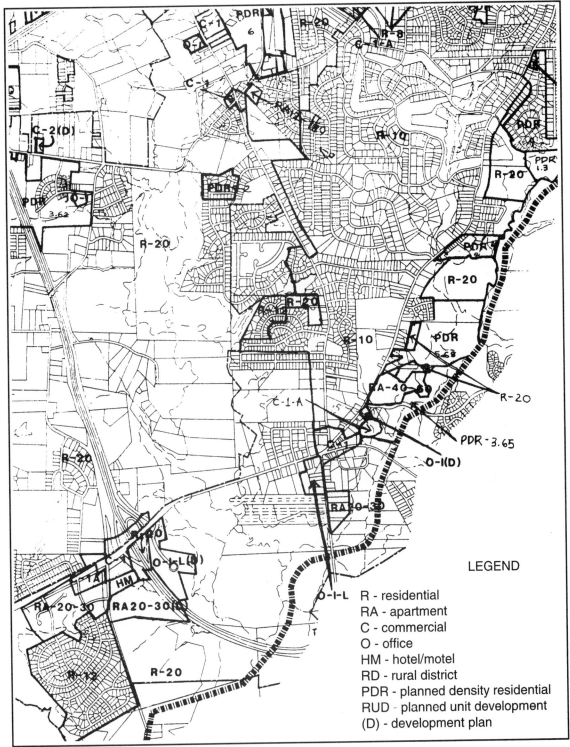

Map 6.2 Zoning in Durham.

LEGEND

R - residential
RA - apartment
C - commercial
O - office
HM - hotel/motel
RD - rural district
PDR - planned density residential
RUD - planned unit development
(D) - development plan

cial. It might prohibit industrial activity in the zone and require that a certain number of parking spaces be built for every 1,000 feet of commercial floor space built.

To develop property that has been zoned, the builder must obtain a permit from the planning department. The planning department staff checks the building plans for the lot to see that all zoning requirements are met. The department then issues a building permit. As building proceeds, inspectors check to see that construction meets the requirements of the state building code. The building code sets standards for safe construction, including plumbing and electrical systems. Inspectors also check to make sure the zoning requirements are being followed. Before the new building can be occupied, inspectors must certify that it meets all state and local requirements, including the zoning regulations.

Zoning applies only to new uses of property. For example, an existing store in an area zoned residential would not be forced to close. However, expanding the store or changing its use to a factory might be prohibited by the zoning ordinance.

Minor exceptions to the zoning regulations can be made by the board of adjustment. This board is appointed by the council or commission. Boards of adjustment for cities with extraterritorial planning jurisdictions must include representatives from that area. The board of adjustment hears appeals about the decisions of the planning staff. It also hears requests for exceptions to the zoning regulations, called **variances**. Board of adjustment decisions usually cannot be appealed to the local governing board. Instead, appeals are made to the courts. This procedure is intended to keep political pressures from influencing land-use decisions.

Because major land-use decisions can affect property values, traffic levels, noise levels, and many other aspects of life in a community, they are frequently controversial. To ensure opportunities for public discussion, major developments such as shopping centers require "special-use permits" which can be granted only after a formal public hearing on the project.

All of North Carolina's larger cities and towns have zoning regulations that the city council has adopted by ordinance. A municipality's zoning authority covers the extraterritorial planning jurisdiction, as well as the area within the municipality. Almost two-thirds of the counties also have zoning for at least some of their area not under municipal jurisdiction. Most of the areas of North Carolina which are not covered by zoning regulation are primarily agricultural, although popular resistance to having local government regulate land use has also prevented the adoption of zoning in some counties where there is considerable industry.

Variance—
permission to do something that is different from what is allowed by current regulations.

an interview with
Richard Petty
County Commissioner
Randolph County

Richard Petty

I guess I've been interested in local government a long time. When I was in school, I got interested in the national side of politics. Eisenhower was President then, but I didn't really think much about county government.

Back in the 1970s, I was president of the Boosters Club in Randleman. All four high schools in the county were going to the school board and the county commissioners for help with improvements in the stadiums. We managed to get a four-year program where the county gave the schools $25,000 each year for things like lights for the stadiums. That was my first introduction to the way county government worked.

I originally decided to run for county commissioner to try to fix some of the problems in my part of the county. I live in the northern part of Randolph County along where Highway 220 comes south out of Greensboro. When I was growing up here, this was strictly a farming community, with some people working in a mill close by. As a matter of fact, our racing shops used to be a farm. When Guilford County (where Greensboro is) started to grow, they started to tighten all their zoning rules. Because Randolph County was not zoned, many kinds of places—like junkyards—moved here to get away from the zoning restrictions. Because there were no zoning rules regarding development, our community was overrun. I got caught up in that issue, because I felt like our community was falling apart.

I said, "Hey, man, you know, there might be something more I could do here." So I called up the chairman of the Republican Party here in the county, and he said, "Why don't you run for county commissioner?"

I wasn't sure if I'd have the time to be on the county commission, but he told me the county commissioners meet on the first Monday of every month and maybe a couple other times during the month. I figured I could take that much time to protect our county—you know what I mean? In the 1978 election, I ran for county commissioner and won. I've been reelected three times since then.

Working on a county commission definitely takes teamwork—just like racing, or football. Although commissioners are in charge in county government, they have to work with the county departments, the school board, and people. We're just there to do what the people think needs to be done. If you're on a county commission, you have to get as much information as you can, talk to as many people as you can, get the lay of the land. You can't give everybody everything they want.

To the students who are reading this book, I just want to say that government is going to be up to you. You're the ones who are going to help make decisions about how the county is going to be run when you're grown up. The sooner you get involved, the more you can control the direction that county government takes. If you don't get involved, then you shouldn't say anything if things don't turn out the way you'd like.

— interviewed by
Roger Schlegel

Subdivision regulations help local governments make sure new housing developments provide adequate building sites and that streets, water, sewers, and other facilities will be available for residents of the new houses.

Subdivision Regulation

Subdivision regulation establishes a process for reviewing a landowner's request to divide a piece of land into building lots. With subdivision regulation, the local government will not approve dividing land into lots for houses until the landowner satisfies certain conditions. These conditions typically include building adequate streets and providing appropriate drainage. The conditions might also include laying water and sewer lines, if the new development is to be served by public water supply and sewers. In addition, each lot must be checked to see that it includes a safe building site. The landowner may also be asked to donate land for a park or **greenspace**. If land is subject to subdivision regulation by local government, the register of deeds cannot record the boundaries of the new lots without approval of the local government. This assures that all regulations are followed.

Subdivision regulation is intended to prevent developments on land that cannot support them (because it floods, for example, or because the soil does not allow septic tanks and no sewers were provided). Subdivision regulation is intended to assure that adequate streets and drainage are provided by the **developer**, so that residents (or the local government) are not left with the expense of building adequate roads or drains. Because many of these problems developed in earlier subdivisions, subdivision regulation is being used more and more. Still, in 1992, more than a third of

Greenspace—
an area that is kept undeveloped to provide more open land in or near a city.

Developer—
a person or business that builds houses or prepares land for building.

North Carolina counties had not adopted subdivision regulations. These were mostly rural counties where little development was occurring.

Minimum Housing Codes

Minimum housing codes establish basic requirements for a place to be "fit for human habitation"—that is, acceptable as someone's living place. Typical requirements include structural soundness (to prevent the collapse of walls or floors), adequate ventilation (to provide the occupants with fresh air), and a safe water supply and toilet facilities (to prevent the spread of disease). If an inspector finds that a building does not meet minimum standards, the inspector can order it to be repaired or closed. A local governing board can adopt an ordinance ordering that a building which is beyond repair be demolished. Most of North Carolina's larger cities and counties have minimum housing codes.

Other Regulations

Other regulations also help protect the physical environment. Local governing boards may regulate community appearance. For example, they can prohibit signs they decide are too large or disturbing. They can regulate changes to the outside appearance of buildings in historic districts. Local governing boards can also protect fragile environments. For example, they may regulate activities that cause soil erosion or regulate building in flood plains or in reservoir watersheds. Like most land-use regulations, ordinances regulating community appearance and environmental protection are usually enforced by building inspectors or by the planning staff.

Local governments also regulate the ways people use public property. They frequently adopt ordinances setting up rules for the use of parks or other facilities open to the public. Cities and towns regulate traffic on their streets. For major thoroughfares (streets that carry traffic into and out of the city) the city or town shares this authority with the state. The city council itself can decide to put up stop signs or traffic signals or to set speed limits on most city streets, but not on some of the busiest. The city council must request state action to regulate traffic on thoroughfares. Because all rural public roads are the state's responsibil-

Computers help officials control traffic lights in Fayetteville to move traffic smoothly through the city.

ity, county governments must ask for state action to control traffic in unincorporated areas. Local and state officials must both approve a thoroughfare plan for all major streets and highways.

USING THE AUTHORITY TO REGULATE

To regulate an activity, the local governing board must first have appropriate authority from the state. Local governments have been given authority to regulate many kinds of behavior. If state law does not already permit local government regulation of an activity, local officials must ask the General Assembly to pass a bill granting that authority. Next, the local governing board must adopt an ordinance. The ordinance is a legal description by the board of the behavior that is being regulated and the actions the government will take against people who do not follow the regulation.

In the News . . .

Residents want growth controlled

By Valerie Thompson
Staff Writer

East Flat Rock—Two of the year's most heated zoning disputes have been tabled by the Henderson County Board of Commissioners, while another has yet to go before the board—much to the chagrin of at least one woman, who says there is no other way to stop the hundreds of mobile homes from moving into her community.

"Anybody can come in and do anything to his property if it is not zoned," Vivian Hill said. "I really feel like this process should be accelerated now. This area (East Flat Rock) is growing by leaps and bounds, and we need some protection. Zoning seems the only way."

Hill is one of several East Flat Rock residents who have asked the county commissioners to zone an approximately two-square-mile area in their community. The

group contends that about 500 mobile homes are located in the unzoned portion of their community, and the number is growing steadily as farmers sell their land to mobile home park developers. Although a Henderson County Planning Board committee has been reviewing the group's request, Hill says she fears all zoning decisions in the county will be postponed until a comprehensive land-use plan can be put into effect.

The county commissioners voted in August to begin work on a comprehensive land-use plan, which should be completed in a year. County Manager David Thompson said the plan is much like a "roadmap for development and preservation."

"It (the land-use plan) sets basic goals in the county: How do we want the county to look in 20 years?" Thompson said.

The land-use plan will not pre-

clude zoning decisions on the part of the commissioners, although they may want to consider whether a decision will be consistent with the land-use plan, Thompson said.

Another hotly contested proposal concerned a request to zone about 1,100 acres of property around Lake Summit.

Lakefront property owners requested residential zoning of the land, citing environmental and safety problems as the basis of their request.

A group of local residents formed a group to fight the zoning proposal—because they feared the zoning would limit public access to the lake.

The commissioners tabled the request in August until the lake-access issue can be resolved.
— adapted from
The Asheville Citizen-Times
October 17, 1991

Frequently people disagree about whether a particular activity is harmful enough to require regulation. Local governing boards often hold public hearings to encourage full discussion of the arguments for and against a proposal to regulate. Sometimes an advisory board or a committee of residents also reviews the arguments about a proposed regulation and presents these to the governing board. People also often speak directly to board members about proposed regulations they particularly favor or oppose. However, the decision to regulate must be made by the local governing board. Unless a majority of the board thinks regulation is appropriate, no action will be taken. Except for a few cities (like Greensboro) that have initiative and referendum, an ordinance can be adopted only by the board.

Governments regulate either by requiring certain actions or by prohibiting certain actions. If someone fails to act according to the requirements of the ordinance, the government can either refuse them certain public services or impose penalties on them. The ordinance specifies what service may be withheld or what penalties may be imposed. Some regulations are enforced by withholding public services until the person acts as the regulation requires. For example, a person who wants to connect his or her home to the public water supply must get permission from the water department. To protect the water supply, local regulations specify the kind of plumbing the owner must install. Then, before the water department turns on the water, an inspector checks the plumbing to be sure it meets specifications.

Frequently, people who violate an ordinance must pay a **civil** penalty of a specified amount of money. When an official enforcing the ordinance determines that a violation has occurred, the official issues a **citation** to the violator, assessing the civil penalty. Sometimes there are other penalties, too. For example, the ordinance regulating parking may include a provision for towing cars parked in parking places reserved for the handicapped. Violations of some ordinances may also carry a fine or time in the county jail. People charged with violating these ordinances have a hearing at which a magistrate or district court judge determines whether they are guilty of the violation and, if so, what their sentence will be.

Police officers are given responsibility for enforcing many local ordinances, but other local officials are also responsible for enforcing specific ordinances. These include fire inspectors, housing inspectors, and zoning inspectors. Often these same local officials are also responsible for enforcing state laws and regulations. Local police enforce North Carolina's criminal laws, as well as local ordi-

Civil—
concerning government's role in relations among citizens. Civil violations are different than criminal violations in that they are not offenses against all the people and are not prosecuted by the district attorney. When governments are involved in civil disputes, they are simply another party in the case, just like a person or a private corporation.

Citation—
an official summons to appear before a court to answer a charge of violating a government regulation.

nances. Local fire inspectors enforce the state fire-prevention code in addition to any local fire-prevention code. Local ordinances must not conflict with state laws and regulations.

Many regulations require popular support to achieve their purposes. For example, most people must cooperate with restrictions on smoking in public places or requirements to keep dogs under control in order for these ordinances to be effective. Police enforcement can help make people aware of the law, but the police cannot be everywhere at once and cannot deal with widespread violations of such ordinances. They have too many other things to do. Fortunately, most people accept their responsibility to obey laws, even when they disagree with the laws. This is the basis for the success of most government regulations.

7 Paying for Local Government

Local government services and programs cost money. Cities and counties have to pay the people who work for them. Local governments must also provide the buildings, equipment, and supplies for conducting public business. They must pay for public services they buy from businesses or community groups. In North Carolina local government services and programs cost billions of dollars each year. In 1991, North Carolina county governments spent more than $4.1 billion, and North Carolina cities and towns spent more than $3.7 billion to provide services for the people of North Carolina.

Within limits set by the state, local officials are responsible for deciding what to spend for local government and how to raise the money to cover those expenses. This chapter focuses on these issues.

Raleigh City Manager Dempsey Benton presents the proposed annual budget to the city council.

A budget is a plan for raising and spending money. North Carolina law requires each city and each county to adopt an annual budget every year, including planned expenditures and **revenues** for the following year. The State of North Carolina sets very strict requirements that local governments must follow in managing their money. That was not always so. During the 1920s many cities and counties in the state borrowed heavily. When the stock market crashed in 1929 and thousands of people lost their jobs, many local governments went even more heavily into debt. By 1931, the state's local governments were spending half of their property tax revenues each year on debt payments. More than half of the state's cities and counties were unable to pay their debts at some time during the Great Depression of the 1930s.

To restore sound money management to local government, the General Assembly created the North Carolina Local Government Commission and passed a series of laws regulating local government budgeting and finance. The Local Government Commission enforces those laws and with the Institute of Government of the University of North Carolina at Chapel Hill provides training and advice to local government budget and finance officers.

State regulation provides a strong framework for sound money management. But local officials still have primary responsibility for using city and county funds wisely and well. During the past 50 years, North Carolina local governments have established a national reputation for managing public money carefully and providing the public with good value for their dollars.

BUDGETING

In North Carolina, local government budgets must be balanced. That is, the budget must indicate that the local government will have sufficient money during the year to pay for all the budgeted expenditures. Expenditures can be paid either from money received during the year (revenue) or from money already on hand at the beginning of the year (**fund balance**). A balanced budget can be represented by the following equation:

Expenditures = Revenues + Fund Balance Withdrawals

Thus, if a local government plans to spend $1 million, it must have a total of $1 million in revenues and fund balance. If it plans to raise only $900,000 in revenue, it needs to be able to withdraw $100,000 from the fund balance. If it plans to raise $950,000, it will need to draw only $50,000 from the fund balance.

The fund balance is like the local government's savings account. It helps the government deal with unexpected situations. Local government revenues are discussed later in the chapter. However, it is important to note here that the budget is based on revenue estimates—educated guesses about how much money the city or county will receive during the coming year. To be safe, local officials usually plan to spend nothing from the fund balance. That is, they budget expenditures equal to estimated revenues. Then, if actual revenues are less than expected, they can withdraw from the fund balance to make up the difference. If revenues exceed actual expenditures, the money is added to the fund balance. If a government regularly withdraws from its fund balance, it will eventually use all its savings and have no "rainy day" money left.

Deciding What to Spend

In North Carolina, annual budgets run from July 1 of one calendar year to June 30 of the following calendar year. This period is called the government's **fiscal year** because it is the year used in accounting for money. ("Fisc" is an old word for treasury.) "Fiscal year" is often abbreviated "FY." FY 1991, for example, means the fiscal year from July 1, 1990, to June 30, 1991. Each year the local

Fiscal year— the twelve-month period used by government for record keeping, budgeting, taxing, and other aspects of financial management.

governing board must adopt the annual budget before the new fiscal year begins on July 1.

Several months before the fiscal year begins, each local government department estimates how much more or less their services will cost in the coming year. For example, if a solid waste collection department is going to continue collecting the same amount of waste from the same number of places at the same frequency, its costs will be about the same. Fuel for the trucks may cost a little more, but if services do not change, next year's expenditures should be quite similar to this year's expenditures. (Raises for employees are often considered sepa-

New services like recycling pick-up add to local governments' expenditures and are new items in the annual budget.

rately from department estimates. They will be discussed later.)

If, in the example, the city council decides to reduce the number of trash collections from twice a week to once a week, the department can reduce the number of employees and the number of miles driven by the trucks. The department will pay less in salaries and fuel bills and perhaps not have to buy replacement trucks as often. The change in services will therefore reduce estimated expenditures for the department.

On the other hand, if the city plans to annex several neighborhoods, the department may need to add trucks and crews to collect solid waste there. These new expenses for additional service will add to estimated expenditures for the department.

After department heads determine how much they think they will need for the next fiscal year, they discuss these estimates with the manager. The manager also looks at expected changes in the other expenditures. For example, health insurance premiums for employees might be expected to increase. Or, employees' salaries might need to be raised so the local government can stay competitive with private employers. In addition to department requests, the manager must add increases that affect all departments.

At the same time, the manager also prepares revenue estimates for the coming year. After all the estimates for both expenditures

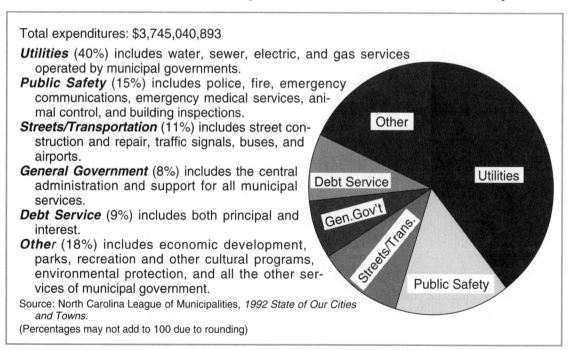

Total expenditures: $3,745,040,893

Utilities (40%) includes water, sewer, electric, and gas services operated by municipal governments.

Public Safety (15%) includes police, fire, emergency communications, emergency medical services, animal control, and building inspections.

Streets/Transportation (11%) includes street construction and repair, traffic signals, buses, and airports.

General Government (8%) includes the central administration and support for all municipal services.

Debt Service (9%) includes both principal and interest.

Other (18%) includes economic development, parks, recreation and other cultural programs, environmental protection, and all the other services of municipal government.

Source: North Carolina League of Municipalities, *1992 State of Our Cities and Towns.*

(Percentages may not add to 100 due to rounding)

Figure 7.1 *Total Expenditures of North Carolina's Cities, Towns, and Villages* 1990–1991 **Fiscal Year**

and revenues are complete, the manager compares the totals. If estimated revenues exceed estimated expenditures, the manager may recommend lowering local tax rates, adding to the fund balance, or beginning new programs and services. If estimated expenditures exceed revenues, the manager may recommend cutting expenditures, raising taxes or fees, or making withdrawals from the fund balance. It is the manager's responsibility to propose a balanced budget to the governing board.

The proposed budget lists the amount of money each department will spend in the coming year. It also lists the amount of money expected from each revenue source for the coming year and the amount the manager proposes to withdraw from (or add to) the fund balance.

The governing board reviews the proposed budget. With the proposed budget is information about the current year's budget, expenditures, and revenues. Council members and commissioners usually pay particularly close attention to proposed changes in spending to decide whether the services their government provides are the best use of public funds. They also pay careful attention to proposals to raise tax rates or the fees people pay for services.

Before the governing board adopts the budget, it must hold a public hearing. This provides people in the community an oppor-

---

Total expenditures: $4,133,976,000

Education (35%) includes the counties' contributions to the public schools and community colleges.

Public Safety (12%) includes sheriff, jail, fire, emergency communications, emergency medical services, animal control, and building inspections.

Human Services (25%) includes public health, mental health, and social services.

General Government (9%) includes the central administration and support for all county services.

Debt Service (6%) includes both principal and interest.

Other (13%) includes economic development, parks, recreation, libraries and other cultural programs, environmental protection, and all the other services of county government.

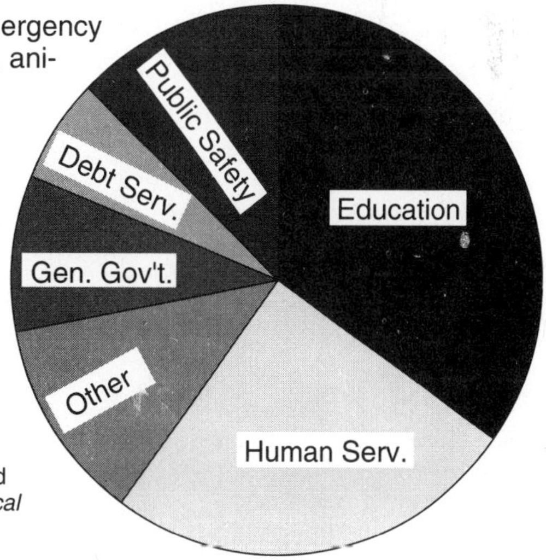

Source: North Carolina Department of the State Treasurer and North Carolina Association of County Commissioners, *Fiscal Summary of North Carolina Counties*, 1991.

(Percentages may not add to 100 due to rounding.)

Figure 7.2 *Total Expenditures of North Carolina's Counties* 1990–1991 Fiscal Year

tunity to express their views about the proposed budget. At any point in its review, the board can change the proposed budget. The annual budget must be adopted by a majority of the board.

Spending Public Funds

In adopting the budget, the governing board formally **appropriates** the expenditures. That is, the board authorizes the amount to be spent for each department during the coming fiscal year. The finance officer keeps records of all expenditures. Before each bill is paid during the year, the finance officer checks to see that there is enough money left in the department's appropriation to pay that bill. Expenditure records also help the manager coordinate government operations and, as we have seen, help in planning the next year's budget. If the government needs to spend more than the amount listed in the budget for a particular purpose, the council (or commission) must pass a budget amendment.

Each local government's budget reflects the choice of services the local governing board has made. Local government budgets also reflect the way the General Assembly has allocated service responsibilities. Most municipalities spend much of their money on utilities, public safety, and streets. Most counties spend a majority of their money on education and human services.

Figures 7.1 and 7.2 show how North Carolina local governments spent their money in the 1990–1991 fiscal year.

Local governments that borrow money to build new facilities must repay what they have borrowed—the **principal**—plus **interest**. Typically, these payments are spread over several years. These payments are called **debt service**. Debt service is often part of local government budgets, for reasons discussed in the following section.

CAPITAL PROJECTS

When a city buys land for a new park or a county builds a new jail or landfill, the project usually costs too much to be paid for from current revenues or from fund balance. Major purchases like land or buildings are called **capital** projects. Local governments usually borrow money to finance large capital projects, although annual revenues or fund balance may be sufficient for small projects.

But borrowing has several disadvantages. Borrowing money is expensive. The borrower (in this case, the city or county) must pay interest to the lender. Borrowing also commits the government to payments on the debt for a period of years, often 20 or more. Debt-service payments need to be included as expenses in each

Appropriate—
to authorize the amounts of money government can spend.

Principal—
the amount of money borrowed.

Interest—
a charge for borrowed money that the borrower agrees to pay the lender.

Debt service—
payments of principal and interest on a loan.

Capital—
facilities used to produce services. Local governments' capital includes land, buildings, equipment, water and sewer lines, city streets and bridges.

annual budget until the debt is paid off.

However, borrowing for capital projects also has advantages. One advantage is that by borrowing, the government can do the project right away. A new landfill or jail may be needed very soon, much sooner than the government would be able to save enough money to pay for the project. Another advantage to starting the project right away is that the costs of land and construction may go up while the government waits for funds to become available. While costs go up, the value of the dollar may go down due to inflation. Inflation helps the borrower, however. Because of inflation, the dollars the government pays back may be worth quite a bit less than the dollars the government borrowed several years earlier. Borrowing for capital projects also places responsibility for paying for the project on those who will use it. Capital projects have many years of useful life. Borrowing spreads out paying for the project over many of those years.

Governments borrow money by issuing **bonds**. Two kinds of bonds are used by North Carolina cities and counties. **General obligation** (G.O.) **bonds** pledge the "faith and credit" of the government. That is, the local government agrees to use tax money if necessary to repay the debt. Bondholders can even require local

Bond—
a loan to government that is made when people buy the government's commitment to repay the loan, plus interest.

General obligation bond—
a loan that a government agrees to repay using tax money, even if the tax rate must be raised.

In the News . . .

Community campaign promoting water bond

By Clarke Morrison
Staff Writer

Proponents and foes of 1989's failed water bond referendum came together Monday in a show of unity for what they said should be a more successful outcome on November 5.

"The community has come together on this issue," Asheville Mayor Ken Michalove told about 50 supporters of a $26 million bond issue to finance improvements to the Asheville-Buncombe water system.

The meeting at the Civic Center to kick off the campaign to promote passage of the referendum began with the playing of "Cool, Clear Water" by The Sons

of the Pioneers. Empty rain barrels provided a touch of symbolism.

Richard Wood, chairman of the Asheville-Buncombe Water Authority, explained that unlike the bond issue two years ago, this one didn't involve a water source.

In 1989 organized opposition surfaced to oppose tapping the French Broad River because of its industrial contaminants. The planned improvements would get more water out of the system's current water sources and solve problems of low pressure that occur during periods of high demand, Wood said.

Most of the bond money would fund expansion of the

capacity of the North Fork water treatment plant, construction of a booster pump station to force more water into distribution lines, and construction of a transmission main into West Asheville.

By law, only Asheville residents can vote in the referendum because the city owns the system, Wood said. However, the improvements will be paid for by all customers of the Water Authority.

Wood said the passage would not require a rate increase beyond 4 percent a year planned through 1997 to account for inflation.
— adapted from
Asheville Citizen-Times
September 17, 1991

governments to raise taxes if that is required to pay the debt. **Revenue bonds** are repaid from revenues the project itself generates. Thus, if a parking deck is built with revenue bonds, the debt is repaid with revenues from fees paid by those who park in the deck.

Under the North Carolina constitution, G.O. bonds cannot be issued unless a majority of the voters approve. A referendum must be held to allow voters to approve or reject all G.O. bonds proposed by city councils or boards of commissioners. G.O. bonds are typically used for nonrevenue-producing projects like schools, courthouses, parks, or jails. Sometimes government officials also prefer to use G.O. bonds for revenue-producing projects like sewer plants, parking decks, or convention centers. This is because G.O. bonds usually have a lower **interest rate** than revenue bonds. Investors feel more secure about the repayment of their money when a bond is backed by local government's power to tax.

The **installment-purchase agreement** is an alternative to borrowing that some governments use. Under this arrangement, someone else (a business or a civic group) builds or buys the facility the government needs. The government then gets to use the facility in return for an annual payment. Unlike rental agreements, however, in this kind of contract, the government is actually buying the property through its payments. Governments can not pledge their taxing power when entering into installment-purchase agreements. The debt is backed by the property being purchased. If the government fails to complete its payments, the facility belongs to those who are leasing it to the government.

REVENUES

Local governments get most of their money from taxes, user fees and charges, and funding from other governments. There are also several smaller revenue sources, including interest the government earns on its the fund balance. The local economy and decisions of state and federal governments play a major part in local government funding. Local officials have only a few ways to increase the amount of revenue their local government receives.

Local Taxes

The **property tax** is the most important local tax. Property taxes are often the largest single source of revenue for a local government, sometimes providing more than half of all revenues. The property tax is based on the **assessed value** of property.

Assessing establishes the value of property for tax purposes. **Real property** (land and the buildings and other improvements on it) is reassessed every eight years. **Personal property** (cars, trucks, business equipment) is reassessed each year. According to North Carolina law, tax assessments are supposed to be at the fair market value of the property. That is, the assessed value should equal the likely sale price of the property. If a property owner thinks an assessed value is too high, he or she may appeal it to the county commissioners when they meet as the "board of equalization and review."

Economic development increases the value of property in a city or a county, thereby increasing its property **tax base**. New real estate developments are assessed as they are completed, so they immediately add to a jurisdiction's **total assessed value**. Unless there is new construction, however, real property is reassessed only every eight years in most counties. The market value of property may change a great deal during the eight years between reassessments.

The **property tax rate** is the amount of tax due for each $100 of assessed value. If a house and lot are valued at $100,000 and the property tax rate is $.90 per $100, the tax due on the property will be $900.

$$\frac{\$100,000}{\$100} = 1,000 \qquad \$.90 \times 1,000 = \$900$$

The property tax is one of the few sources of revenue the local governing board can influence directly. For that reason, setting the property tax rate is often the last part of budget review. To set the rate, local officials must first determine how much the city or

In the News . . .

County Moves to Collect Unpaid Taxes

Delinquent taxpayers in Alleghany County will have something to worry about in the next 18 months.

The county Board of Commissioners on October 7 authorized County Attorney Richard Doughton and Tax Administrator Ronald W. Norman to proceed with the collection process, which could result in foreclosure two years from the tax due date.

A list of delinquencies was published in May as required by state law.

Doughton said the county would first send letters to delinquent taxpayers, warning them that they would be taken to court, to give them an opportunity to pay their tax and penalties and avoid court costs.

Delinquent taxpayers are liable for all the costs incurred in collecting the taxes.

He noted that some taxpayers owing for several years might be difficult to find, especially if the original owner is deceased and the county has to track down heirs or appoint guardians. But, he said, the only way to get such land back on the tax rolls is "to put it back in the hands of someone who's going to pay it."

The entire foreclosure process takes two years.
— adapted from
The Alleghany News
October 17, 1991

county needs to raise in property taxes to balance the budget. All other estimated revenues are added together. That figure is subtracted from the total expenses the local government plans to have. The balance is the amount that must be raised through property taxes.

To set the property tax rate, the amount which the government must raise through property taxes is divided by the total assessed value of property in the jurisdiction. That gives the amount of tax which needs to be raised for each dollar of assessed value. To get the tax rate per $100 of assessed value, we multiply by 100. For example, if a city has a total assessed value of $500 million and needs to raise $4 million from property taxes, its property tax rate would be $.80 per $100 of assessed value.

$$\frac{\$4,000,000}{\$500,000,000} = .008 \qquad .008 \times \$100 = \$.80$$

The higher the assessed value of taxable property, the lower the tax rate needed to produce a given amount of revenue. If the assessed value of property in our example above were $600 million, the city could raise $4 million from property taxes with a property tax rate of only $.67 per $100 of assessed value.

The property tax rate for the next fiscal year is set by the local governing board when it adopts the annual budget. Sometimes there is considerable controversy over raising the property tax rate. Many people are quite aware of the property tax. Property owners get a bill from the local tax collector for the entire amount each year. Thus, people know exactly how much they pay in local property tax. (In contrast, the sales tax is collected a few pennies or a few dollars at a time. Most people lose track of how much they pay in sales tax.) Also, the connection between the property tax and the services government provides may be difficult to see. After all, people get public services all year long, but the property tax bill comes only once a year.

Most property owners pay their taxes. In North Carolina, more than 95 percent of all property taxes are typically paid each year. When taxes on property are not paid, the government can go to court to take the property and order it sold to pay the tax bill.

Property tax bills are sent out in August, early in the new fiscal year, yet no penalties for late payment are imposed until January. Therefore, most people wait until December to pay their property taxes. Local governments must pay their bills each month. They cannot wait until they have received property tax payments to pay their employees and suppliers. This is another reason the fund balance is important. Local governments need to have money on hand to pay their bills while they wait for property taxes to be paid.

Local governments may also levy a variety of other taxes, including taxes for the privilege of doing business, keeping a dog or other pet or keeping an automobile inside city limits. The General Assembly limits the amount of these taxes, usually to a few dollars each.

State-Collected Taxes

The **sales tax** provides a substantial part of most local governments' revenues. State law permits each county to levy a tax of $.02 on each dollar of sales in the county, and all the counties do so. (The state levies an additional $.04.) Businesses collect the money from their customers each time the customer pays for a purchase. The state collects sales tax receipts from businesses throughout North Carolina and then returns the local portion of the sales tax to the cities and counties.

Sales tax revenues are divided between county and municipal governments according to formulas established by the General Assembly. Each board of county commissioners decides whether sales tax revenues will be divided with that county's municipalities on the basis of a population formula or on the basis of the amount of taxes collected in each jurisdiction. City councils have no control over how much sales tax revenue they receive, and county commissioners can only decide whether to divide sales tax receipts with cities either according to population or according to where the tax was paid. Only the state legislature can raise the sales tax rate. Neither city nor county officials have control over how much money the sales tax produces for local government.

Because the sales tax rate is set by the General Assembly, the amount of revenue in any year depends on economic conditions. The more people spend on purchases, the greater the sales tax revenue. When the economy slows down and people buy less, sales tax

Sales tax—
a tax on each purchase paid by the buyer at the time of purchase.

The State of North Carolina shares gasoline taxes with municipalities to help them pay for street repairs. Cities also use these "Powell Bill" funds to pay for new street construction.

revenues go down, too.

North Carolina has a separate tax on the sale of gasoline. A part of the state **gasoline tax** is distributed to each municipality in the state. This money, called **"Powell Bill"** funds, can be used only for the construction and maintenance of city streets. In FY 1991, almost $82 million dollars in Powell Bill funds were transferred from the state to North Carolina cities and towns.

Because the gasoline tax is a tax on each gallon of gasoline pur-chased, when gasoline prices go up and people buy less gasoline, Powell Bill funds go down. This leaves cities with less money for streets.

Cities and counties also receive money from the state for a vari-ety of taxes on such things as stocks and bonds, electricity and tele-phone service, and beer and wine sales. The state also pays local governments money to replace some of the revenue lost when the state removed some property from the local tax base. Local officials have no control over these revenues, however. The General Assembly sets these tax rates and determines how the funds will be distributed.

User Fees

Local governments charge customers for many of the services they use. These charges are called "user fees." You pay a fee to swim at the public pool or play golf at the public park. You pay a fare to ride on the city bus. Cities and counties with public water supplies and sewer sys-tems charge water and sewer customers based on the amount of water used. Some North Carolina cities also operate the local electric service and charge customers for the electricity they use. These charges are all based on the cost of providing the service. The people who use these services help to pay for the direct ben-efits they get from them.

A representative of Rocky Mount's municipal electric utility dis-cusses ways to save money by making home improvements to reduce the use of electricity.

In many cases, the users do not pay the entire cost of providing the service, however. Governments **subsidize** services because the public also benefits from the service. For example, city bus fares are usually heavily subsidized because having people travel on buses reduces the number of cars on the streets. Bus riders reduce traffic congestion and parking problems for those who do drive cars. Bus riders reduce the need for new street and parking construction.

Local governing boards have the authority to set user fees. Next to the property tax, user fees are the largest source of local government revenue that local officials can control. As local governments have been asked to do more, local officials in many jurisdictions have begun to rely more on user fees to raise the necessary revenue. Fees for collecting solid waste have been established. Fees for building inspections and other regulation have also been increased to cover more of the costs of conducting these regulatory activities.

Increased reliance on user fees means that more of the cost of public service is paid directly by the customer who gets the service. Less is paid as a **subsidy** from other sources, and so the cost for each user goes up. When the public has a great interest in seeing that everyone gets the service, regardless of ability to pay, user fees set at the full cost of service may mean that public benefits are lost. For example, if bus riders have to pay the full cost of buying and operating the buses, fares may be so high that most riders choose to have their own cars, adding to traffic congestion and the need for more street and parking construction.

Subsidize—
to reduce the amount users pay for a service by funding some of the cost from another source.

Subsidy—
a payment which reduces the cost to the user.

Bus riders pay only a part of the cost of providing bus service. City and federal tax funds help subsidize bus service. The public benefits from bus ridership through decreased traffic congestion.

An Interview with
Gwen C. Burton
Wilson City Council Member

Gwen Burton is a member of the Wilson City Council.

The shortage of money is the most pressing problem facing Wilson and many other cities across North Carolina. During the last decade, cities have seen increased federal and state mandates. At the same time, federal and state funding to cities has decreased. Elected officials of all parties, at all levels of government have been reluctant to raise taxes. We have ever-increasing demands for city services and fewer and fewer resources with which to pay for them.

In Wilson, we have been luckier than many other cities. Our utilities revenue has given us some flexibility and cushion in tough economic times. We haven't yet been forced to make as many really tough decisions as some cities. Nevertheless, we are forced to make choices. Council members are not always in agreement about what we should choose to do.

People expect so much more from city government than they used to. When citizens demand an increase in basic life-safety services—more police, for example—we simply get them more. Citizens have a right to basic life-safety protection: firefighting, police service, clean water.

Beyond that, citizens have to understand that they get what they pay for. They need to know what their tax rate is, and that their electric bill pays for lots of city services, while keeping their tax rate artificially low.

Once they understand where these tax and utility dollars are going, then they must decide how much a particular service is worth. We have lots of requests for lowering tax and utility bills, but we almost never have a request for reduced services.

If I believe in something strongly enough, I'll fight to the wire for it. But we all have to be prepared sometimes to compromise or delay "pet projects" in favor of the greater good. I think we all know we have enough money right now to do the things we really need to do for our citizens. It is our responsibility to be good stewards of the taxpayers' money. Healthy debate among councilmembers about fiscal and other policy matters helps ensure that we are.

— interviewed by
  Marcy Onieal

State and Federal Aid

Local governments get some of their revenue from state and federal governments. Grants and other aid programs help local governments meet specific needs. During the 1960s and 1970s, **intergovernmental assistance** was a major source of local revenue. During the 1980s, many federal grant programs were abolished or greatly reduced and intergovernmental assistance became a much smaller part of local government revenues. However, several important aid programs remain.

Community Development Block Grants help cities and counties improve housing, public facilities, and economic opportunities in low income areas. Projects funded under this federal program include installation of water and sewer lines, street paving, housing rehabilitation, and other community improvements.

Many social service benefits, such as Aid to Families with Dependent Children, Medicaid, and Food Stamps are paid largely with federal funds. State grants also help to pay for some of the costs of social service programs. Local employees administer these programs. They determine who is eligible and see that appropriate benefits get to those who qualify. Counties also get some federal and state funds to help pay these administrative costs for social service programs, although most of the administrative costs must be paid from county funds.

State and federal funds are also provided to counties to support health and mental health services. A complex set of programs and regulations governs the way these funds are used.

Other Local Revenues

When a city or county extends water and sewer lines to new areas, the owners of the property getting the new lines typically pay the local government a special **assessment**. The assessment helps cover the cost of constructing the new lines. Having public water supplies and sewer service available to the property increases its market value, so the owner is charged for the improvement. Similarly, cities usually charge property owners along a street for the cost of paving the street or installing sidewalks along it.

Interest earned on the fund balance can be another important revenue source. Most local governments try to maintain a fund balance equal to 15 to 20 percent of annual expenditures. This provides a ready source of funding for months when tax collections are slow. A sizable fund balance can also help cover an unexpected decrease in revenues. (Remember, local officials have little control over most of their revenues and cannot change the property tax rate they adopt with the annual budget.) Until the funds are

Intergovernmental assistance—money given to local governments by state and federal governments to help meet specific needs.

Assessment—a charge imposed on property owners for building streets, sidewalks, water lines, sewers, or other improvements government makes to the property.

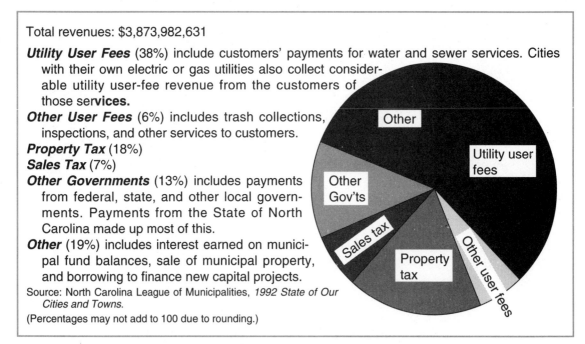

Total revenues: $3,873,982,631

Utility User Fees (38%) include customers' payments for water and sewer services. Cities with their own electric or gas utilities also collect considerable utility user-fee revenue from the customers of those services.

Other User Fees (6%) includes trash collections, inspections, and other services to customers.

Property Tax (18%)

Sales Tax (7%)

Other Governments (13%) includes payments from federal, state, and other local governments. Payments from the State of North Carolina made up most of this.

Other (19%) includes interest earned on municipal fund balances, sale of municipal property, and borrowing to finance new capital projects.

Source: North Carolina League of Municipalities, *1992 State of Our Cities and Towns.*

(Percentages may not add to 100 due to rounding.)

Figure 7.3   Total Revenues for North Carolina's Cities, Towns, and Villages 1990–1991 Fiscal Year

needed, the fund balance can be invested and the interest added to government revenues.

For most municipalities, utility user fees are the biggest source of revenue. Property taxes are the county's largest source of revenue. Figures 7.3 and 7.4 show the various sources for FY 1991 municipal and county revenues.

REPORT TO THE PEOPLE

At the end of each fiscal year, every local government in North Carolina prepares an annual financial report. This document summarizes all of the government's financial activity: what it has received, what it has borrowed, what it has spent, what it is obligated to spend, and what it has in the fund balance. Each local government publishes its annual financial report, has it audited by an independent accounting firm, and files a financial summary with the Local Government Commission.

Preparation of the report helps local officials better understand the financial situation of their government. The independent audit and the report to the Local Government Commission serve as checks on the accuracy of the report and the legality of the government's financial dealings. And the publication of the report informs citizens about their local government's financial condition.

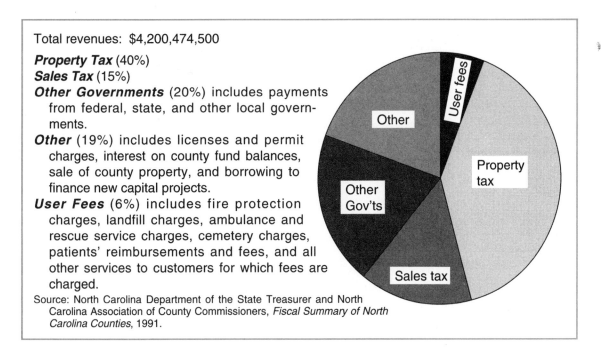

Total revenues: $4,200,474,500

Property Tax (40%)
Sales Tax (15%)
Other Governments (20%) includes payments from federal, state, and other local governments.
Other (19%) includes licenses and permit charges, interest on county fund balances, sale of county property, and borrowing to finance new capital projects.
User Fees (6%) includes fire protection charges, landfill charges, ambulance and rescue service charges, cemetery charges, patients' reimbursements and fees, and all other services to customers for which fees are charged.

Source: North Carolina Department of the State Treasurer and North Carolina Association of County Commissioners, *Fiscal Summary of North Carolina Counties*, 1991.

Figure 7.4 Total Revenues for North Carolina's Counties 1990–1991 Fiscal Year

8 Making Government Work

Good government does not just happen. Good government is the result of people working together to decide what needs to be done for the community and then working to carry out those decisions. People make government work.

Who are the people involved in local government? This chapter explores the answer to that question. We consider six groups: local government employees, volunteers, elected officials, members of appointed boards, voters, and the general public.

People may be in several of these groups at once. For example, all voters are members of the general public, and all elected officials are also voters. Government employees may also be volunteers in other public agencies. They are almost always voters, too. This chapter discusses the different groups separately to indicate the different ways people help shape the way government works.

LOCAL GOVERNMENT EMPLOYEES

Counties and municipalities hire many different kinds of workers. Counties hire nurses, social workers, sanitation inspectors, librarians, and many other specialists to perform county services. Similarly, cities hire police officers, engineers, machinery operators, recreation supervisors, and a wide variety of other specialists to carry out their services. In addition, both city and county governments hire accountants, clerks, maintenance workers, secretaries, administrators, and other staff to support the work of the government. These employees organize government activities, keep government records and accounts of public money, clean and repair government property, and pay the government's bills.

North Carolina counties employed nearly 41,000 people in 1991. Cities and towns in North Carolina employed another 36,000. Local governments thus employed, on average, about 12 people for every 1,000 residents of the state.

Firefighters are among the many local government employees serving the people of North Carolina.

Nepotism—
hiring or giving favorable treatment to an employee because he or she is a member of one's family.

Favoritism—
hiring or giving favorable treatment to an employee because of friendship.

Patronage—
hiring or giving favorable treatment to an employee because he or she is a member of one's political party.

Merit—
hiring or promoting based on a person's ability to do the job or performance on the job.

Most North Carolina local governments have well-established systems for hiring employees on the basis of their qualifications for the job. In some other states, people who work for local government sometimes get their jobs because of personal or political connections. Hiring based on family is called **nepotism**, hiring based on friendship is called **favoritism**, and hiring based on political support is called **patronage**. Most North Carolina local governments have and enforce rules against nepotism, favoritism, and patronage. Instead, local governments in North Carolina usually hire people who have the training and experience to do well the job they are being hired for. This is known as hiring based on **merit**. Local governments in North Carolina hire people on the basis of merit because their primary concern is having employees who can provide the best government services for the lowest cost.

In a merit system, people are also promoted or dismissed on the basis of their job performance, rather than for personal or political reasons. That is, employees who perform their jobs well and show ability for new responsibilities get promoted. Those who do their jobs adequately keep them. And those who do not do an acceptable job get fired.

Except in the smallest North Carolina local governments, the governing board appoints a manager who is responsible for hiring, promoting, and dismissing government employees. The board judges the manager on how well services are provided and how well government funds are used. Thus, the manager wants to be sure that employees are doing their jobs well.

In larger counties and cities, the manager assigns much of the work of hiring and supporting the government's employees to a personnel department. To guide its work, the personnel department prepares job descriptions for all employees.

An employee's job description lists the duties of the job. When a job becomes vacant, the local government uses the job description to advertise the position. The personnel department accepts job applications from people who would like to be hired for the vacant position. In filling out the job application, the applicant lists his or her education, job training, skills, and previous work experience. The personnel department reviews the applications and selects the applicants who appear to be best qualified for the job. For some jobs, applicants are given a test to see how well qualified they are. Applicants are often asked to provide the names of **references**. The references are asked for their judgments about the applicant's qualifications for the job. The final set of applicants are then interviewed, usually by the person who would supervise their work if they were hired. That person is usually responsible for recommending who gets hired.

References— people who know how well someone did on a previous job or about that person's other qualifications for a job.

Most local government employees get much satisfaction from working for the public. They are honest, hard-working people who care about making their community a better place. Occasionally, some government employee takes advantage of the public trust and uses his or her government job to cheat the public. Because they are quite rare, these cases get a lot of attention in the press. Most city and county employees in North Carolina take pride in working for the public and in doing their best to see that government programs are well carried out.

VOLUNTEERS

Volunteers also help carry out important public services. In many places in North Carolina, volunteers fight fires and provide emergency rescue services. Volunteers assist in programs for young people, the elderly, the homeless, and other groups with special needs. The volunteers may be organized through a city or county's fire department, recreation department, social services department, or other division of government. Or the volunteers may be organized through a non-profit corporation which works in cooperation with local government.

Like their full-time, paid counterparts, volunteer firefighters and emergency medical service technicians are required to have exten-

Volunteers deliver many public services in cooperation with local governments. Here volunteers are welcomed to a celebration in their honor.

sive training and are well-qualified to do their jobs. In fact, most of the unincorporated areas of the state and most of the small municipalities depend on volunteers for fire fighting. Also, many counties rely on volunteer emergency rescue squads to provide medical assistance and rescue work.

Many volunteer fire departments are organized as nonprofit associations. They have contracts with a local government to provide fire protection to a specific area. The volunteer fire department receives public funds to buy equipment and supplies needed in fighting fires. Similarly, municipal and county governments often provide buildings or funding for emergency shelters, senior citizen centers, hot lunch programs, youth recreation leagues, and other services operated by nonprofit organizations and staffed by volunteers.

Volunteers enjoy the work they do. They get satisfaction from doing the work itself. They get pleasure from working with other volunteers. And they have the rewards of knowing they have helped other people and improved the community. By volunteering for public service, students, retirees, and people who work full time in other jobs share some of the special pride of working for the good of the community.

ELECTED OFFICIALS

The elected leaders of local governments are the members of their governing boards. For counties, these are the county commissioners. For municipalities, they are the council members (or "aldermen" or commissioners) and mayor. These officials have the authority to adopt policies for local government and are responsible to the people for seeing that local government responds to public needs and works well to meet those needs.

The governing board is the local government's legislature. The members discuss and debate policy proposals. Under state law, the board has the authority to determine what local public services to provide, what community improvements to pursue, and what kinds of behavior and land use to regulate as harmful. The local governing board also sets local tax rates and user fees and adopts a budget for spending the local government's funds. The board appoints the manager who is chief administrator for the government. All of these are group decisions. The board votes, and a majority must approve any action.

Each local governing board has a presiding officer—someone who conducts the meetings of the governing board, speaks officially for the local government, and represents the government at ceremonies and celebrations. In cities and towns, this is the mayor. Voters elect the mayor in most North Carolina cities and towns. In a few of the state's municipalities, however, members of the local governing board elect a mayor from among the members of the board. The presiding officer for a county is the chairman of the board of county commissioners. (Although the office is officially called "chairman," women can and do hold the office.) In most North Carolina counties, the board elects one of its members as chairman. In one county, the voters elect the chairman of the board of county commissioners.

The sheriff and the register of deeds are elected to head their respective departments of county government. The state constitution requires that these two officials be elected in each North Carolina county. The sheriff's department operates the county jail, patrols and investigates crimes in areas of the county not served by other local police departments, and serves court orders and subpoenas. The register of deeds office maintains official records of land and of births, deaths, and marriages. Both the sheriff and the register of deeds hire their own staffs. They are not required to hire on the basis of merit, although their employees must meet basic requirements set by the state.

School boards are also local governing boards. They are like city and county governing boards, except their authority is more limited. They are responsible only for policies regarding the local public schools, and they cannot set tax rates or appropriate funds. The county commissioners determine how much money the county will spend to support local public schools.

an interview with
Vernon Malone
Chairman, Board of County Commissioners
Wake County

I guess my getting into politics was more by accident than by design. I never originally decided I wanted to be the next President of the United States or governor or constable. I never had any of those grand goals. I drifted into this accidentally, more or less.

When I was in college here—I grew up in Raleigh and have lived in this area all my life—I was an avid reader. One of the things that aggravated me a great deal when I was a college student was the way the press would vilify certain segments of the population as opposed to the way they treated other segments of the population for the same "offense." For example, back in my era, there was a very, very keen rivalry between the black high school in Raleigh and the black high school in Durham. The two schools almost always ended football games with a melee—loud yelling, fisticuffs, and so forth. There was a similar rivalry between Broughton High School in Raleigh and Durham High School—both white schools. If anything went on between the white high schools, it was always buried in the back part of the paper near the classified ads. But if anything went on between the black high schools, it made the front page of the *News and Observer*. That always aggravated me. I became very vocal on that issue.

By the time I had children of my own, school integration was a major issue. The people who chartered the new school system seemed to cater only to the wishes of white students and their parents. We had to accept whatever their rulings were, and I challenged them. When a good friend of mine was elected to a position on the Board of County Commissioners, I was appointed to fill her vacant seat on the Board of

Vernon Malone presides at a meeting of the Wake County Board of Commissioners

Education. I served on that board for about 13 years, having been reelected for several terms. In 1988 I was encouraged to seek a seat on the Board of Commissioners, and I was elected. So here I am.

I guess it's sort of being at the right place at the "wrong" time that got me into politics. It was nothing I ever set out to do. I still don't see the job as glamorous. I see it as laborious, painful, and time-consuming. It's awfully difficult to have the responsibility of regulating the lives of people, but that is the business I'm in. Every single decision I make has either a negative or positive impact on somebody's life in this community. I have to weigh that when I make a decision, and I have to live with it.

I would recommend public service to anyone who is genuinely interested in serving rather than being served. If you want to serve for your own personal gratification, then stay away from the courthouse. If you really are interested in the problems on the street and would like to be a part of the solution, then yes. We need good professional county and city managers. We need talented sheriffs and chiefs of police. We need good solid-thinking council members and commissioners—people who are able to look globally at a broad range of issues and who don't have narrow personal interests.

"You've got to stay in school." That's my message. Know what's going on. Understand how our government works. Know what the issues are and be able to sift through the rhetoric to get right to the heart of issues. The only way to do all that is to have a wealth of knowledge. Study. Study government. Study the people in government. Look at the issues and determine whether government is setting the right priorities.

Local government meetings should be filled with student voices. Students can organize vol-unteer groups to help with recycling or health care. Students can organize letter-writing campaigns. We would love to hear from you. Invite elected officials to your school for question and answer sessions on current issues. Ask them different questions. We can learn from you. Students bring their own concerns, and they mirror the feelings and concerns of their parents as well. In my experience, students not only bring issues to us, but they in turn can carry information back home. Students have a unique opportunity to educate their own families in the political process.

—interviewed by
Marcy Onieal

All local elected officials represent the people of the jurisdiction. People often contact these elected officials to suggest policy changes or to express their opinions on policy proposals that are being considered by the board. Boards hold public hearings on particularly controversial issues to provide additional opportunities for people to tell the board their views on policy proposals.

Elected officials get their authority from the people. Campaigning for office gives candidates an opportunity to express their views about local issues and to hear what citizens want from their elected officials. Elections give voters the opportunity to choose candidates who share their views on issues. Through election, voters give elected officials the authority to make decisions which everyone will have to obey. Through election, voters also hold elected officials accountable. People can vote against an elected official who does not represent them and defeat that official in the next election.

Elections are held every two or four years, depending upon the term of office established for each office. In jurisdictions where board members are elected by district or **ward**, each voter votes only for the candidate from the voter's own district. In jurisdictions where members are elected at large, each voter may vote for as many candidates as there are positions to be filled. (Some jurisdictions have at-large elections for board members, but require that candidates live in and run for seats representing specific dis-

Ward—
a section of a jurisdiction for voting, representative, or administrative purposes.

tricts.) Election by district may produce a more diverse governing board if minority groups are concentrated in some parts of the jurisdiction. Districts can be drawn around those population concentrations so that a group which is a minority in the total population is a majority within the district. Federal courts have required district elections in counties and municipalities which have substantial African American populations but have failed to elect African American board members.

Elections for county commissioners are held on the Tuesday after the first Monday in November in even-numbered years, along with elections for state officials and members of Congress. The county sheriff and register of deeds are elected then, too. In practice, the sheriff and register of deeds are often reelected, term after term. Often, sheriffs and registers of deeds serve until they choose to retire. Frequently their successors have served as their deputies. Sometimes, however, these elections are highly contested—especially the elections for sheriff.

County elections are **partisan**. That is, candidates run under **political party** labels. Primary elections are held several months before the November general election. Primary elections are elections among the candidates of a party to choose the party's candidates for the general election. In the primary election, members of each party vote only for their party's candidate. The two major political parties are the Democratic Party and the Republican Party. Other parties and non-party candidates may also get on the ballot by filing petitions.

Partisan—
involving political parties
Political party—
a group of people who organize to win elections, operate government, and make public policy.

Elections for city council members (or aldermen) are held in odd-numbered years. Election for mayor is held at the same time in those cities and towns where the voters elect the mayor. Most cities and towns have nonpartisan elections. That is, candidates do not run under party labels. These municipalities may have local voters' organizations that support candidates, but the Democratic and Republican parties are not

Rocky Mount city council members and mayor displayed the city's new flag in 1992.

permitted to run candidates in most North Carolina municipalities. Only a few cities and towns hold primary elections.

Most school board elections are also nonpartisan. School board elections are in even-numbered years, with some at the time of the general election, some at the time of the primary election, and some on other, special election dates.

Altogether, more than 700 elected officials serve the state's county governments and almost 3,000 elected officials serve in North Carolina municipalities.

Why do people run for a seat on the local governing board? They may be interested in getting local government to adopt a particular policy proposal. They may want to help shape the future of the community more generally. They may feel an obligation to serve the public. They may want to explore politics and perhaps prepare for seeking state or federal office. They may enjoy exercising public responsibility or being recognized as a public leader.

MEMBERS OF APPOINTED BOARDS

Local governments also have appointed boards or commissions. These provide opportunities for many other citizens to assist the elected governing board in shaping public policy. State law requires that some of these (such as Alcoholic Beverage Control boards, and boards of elections, health, mental health, and social services) play a direct role in selecting agency heads and setting operating policies for the agency. Other boards are established by the local government to provide policy direction for airports, civic centers, public housing, stadiums, or other public facilities. Still other boards advise elected officials directly on matters ranging from the environment to human relations, from recreation to job training, from open space to transportation. Large cities and counties may have more than thirty appointed boards and commissions, and many hundreds of citizens may serve on the boards of a large local government.

In many cases, at least some of the members of an appointed board must be selected from specific groups in the community. For example, a mental health board must include, among others, a physician, an attorney, and a "primary consumer in recovery and representing the interests of individuals with drug abuse." Other boards and commissions may require that members be residents of various parts of the jurisdiction to provide broad geographic representation. County boards of elections must include both Democrats and Republicans, with the party of the Governor having the majority of members.

People volunteer to serve on appointed boards and commissions for many of the same reasons people run for election. Having a particular concern for the subject the board deals with is especially important for many volunteers. Appointed boards have a narrower range of concerns than city councils or county commissions. Appointed boards provide an opportunity for people with a particular interest in historic preservation or nursing homes or another specific public policy area to work on policy for that particular concern.

VOTERS

The voters in each jurisdiction choose the members of their local governing boards. The voters in each county also elect a sheriff and a register of deeds. The voters must also approve any agreement by their local government to borrow money that will be repaid with tax receipts. Through voting, the people determine who their government leaders will be and give the officials they elect the authority to govern. Voting is, thus, the essential act of representative democracy. Voting is both a very special responsibility and a very important civil right.

Who can vote?

Struggles over the right to vote have continued ever since the United States gained independence from Great Britain. At independence, only free male citizens who were 21 years of age or older and who paid taxes could vote for members of the lower house of

A Guilford County voter examines the ballot before she closes the curtain to vote.

the North Carolina General Assembly. Only men who met all those qualifications and also owned at least 50 acres of land could vote for members of the state senate. (There were no local elected officials.) Most African Americans were held as slaves and could not vote at all. In 1835 the General Assembly prohibited even free men of African descent from voting in North Carolina.

The Civil War ended slavery, and in 1870 the Fifteenth Amendment to the United States Constitution extended voting rights to all male citizens 21 or older, regardless of "race, creed, color, or previous condition of servitude." For the next few years, African Americans were able to vote as the Constitution permitted. In 1890 more than 1,000 black North Carolinians held office. But some white leaders feared an alliance between black voters and poor white voters. To prevent that alliance, some white leaders stirred up racial fears among whites and pushed racial segregation. The segregation laws were called "Jim Crow" laws. By the end of the nineteenth century, the North Carolina General Assembly had devised means of keeping most nonwhite men from voting, and the federal government refused to enforce the Constitution.

Women could not vote in North Carolina at the beginning of the twentieth century either, even though some people had long been seeking voting rights (or "suffrage") for women. Finally, in 1920 the women's suffrage movement was successful. That year the Nineteenth Amendment to the United States Constitution extended the right to vote to female citizens 21 and older.

Although white women began to vote in North Carolina in the 1920s, most African American and Native American citizens of North Carolina were kept from voting until the 1960s. A major accomplishment of the civil rights movement, which also ended racial segregation in North Carolina, was the guarantee of voting rights for all adult citizens.

The last extension of voting rights came in 1971 when the Twenty-sixth Amendment to the United States Constitution guaranteed the right to vote to younger adults. Now all citizens who are at least 18 years old are eligible to vote. Anyone who was born in the United States is a citizen. So are children born in other countries if either of their parents is a United States citizen. Other people who are born in other countries may become United States citizens through naturalization, a procedure administered by the U.S. State Department.

Being eligible to vote does not make you a voter, however. To be a voter, you must first register with the local board of elections in the county where you live. Seventeen-year-old citizens may register if they will be eighteen years old by the next general election. Thus, you can register and vote in a primary election when you are seventeen if your eighteenth birthday comes before the November general election. To be a voter, of course, you must also cast your **ballot**—that is, you must vote!

Each county is divided into voting **precincts**. The county board of elections establishes a place to vote—a **polling place**—in each precinct. Registered voters may cast their ballots in person at the polling place on election day. If they are unable to get to the polling place because of illness or travel, they may vote by **absentee ballot**.

People vote because they want to exercise their rights. They vote to support candidates, parties, or issues. They vote to oppose candidates, parties, or issues. They vote to make their communities better. They vote to show that the government belongs to them and because they feel responsible for helping to select public leaders.

THE GENERAL PUBLIC

Everyone uses local government services. Everyone is affected by the decisions local government makes. Everyone also influences local government decisions. Sometimes people are not aware of how they are influencing public policy. Other times they might be trying very hard to change local government policies.

People unintentionally influence local government policies through the use of government services, through their cooperation (or noncooperation) with government programs, and through public behavior that harms others.

How does using government services affect public policy? Government officials often consider use to indicate public wants or needs. According to this view, the more people use a service, the more of that service the government should try to provide. Of course, local governments may not be able to increase the service, or officials may decide they cannot afford to do so. In such a situation, officials may try to limit use, but limiting use is also a government policy.

For example, the more often people use a ball field, the fewer hours it is available for other users. Government officials might respond to this increase in use by putting up lights so the field could also be used at night. Or they might build additional fields so that more teams can play at the same time. These are examples of adding more service in response to increased use. But the local governing board might decide it could not afford to add lights or new fields or that adding them would cause other public prob-

City allows 'play street'

By Brad Rich
Staff Writer

Approximately 80 colorfully clad skateboarders, including one with greenish hair, got what they wanted from the Morehead City Council Tuesday night: a street to use as a temporary safe haven and a council commitment to find a long-term solution to the skateboard "problem."

The council, during a meeting in the municipal building, designated South 3rd Street as a temporary "play street," which means motorists and the board enthusiasts must share the asphalt.

The council also appointed a committee to look into construction of a skateboard park or other solutions, such as permanent designation of "play streets" that skateboarders could use during certain hours.

Skateboards technically are banned on city streets, and coun-cilmen, fearing for the safety of skateboarders and motorists and pedestrians who share the city streets and sidewalks, earlier this month directed the city's legal council to draft an ordinance to ban the hot wheels from the side-walks.

That ordinance was drafted and presented before the council Tuesday, as was a report by City Manager David Walker that outlined liability and other problems at a skateboard park in Havelock.

But faced with skateboarders, who promised to practice their sport, ordinance or no ordinance, and parents who praised the kids and decried the potential demise of their favorite pastime, the council ditched the draft.

By unanimous vote, South 3rd Street was designated a "play street." The short street, at the eastern end of the city limits, runs from Arendell Street to the water-front, between Leeward Harbor and the Dockside condominiums.

Signs will be posted warning motorists of the designation. Councilmen urged skateboarders to cooperate with motorists who must still use the street to get to the condominiums.

The committee will be under the auspices of the city recreation committee, and will include at least two skateboarders, two of their parents, two councilmen, two recreation committee members, and the city police chief, Ken Bumgarner.

The council acted after hearing from several parents, a representative of a surf shop that sells skateboards, and one youthful skateboarder.

— adapted from
Carteret County News-Times
November 27, 1991

lems. Instead, officials might decide to limit use of the existing field. They might require people who want to use the field to reserve it in advance or to pay a fee or join a league that schedules games on the field. These are all ways of rationing the service. Rationing is also a response to increased use, but a response which limits use instead of adding service.

Cooperating or failing to cooperate with government programs also influences public policy in important ways. Many programs can succeed only if people cooperate. If they do not, government officials will have to redesign the program in order to handle the problem in another way. Consider the problem of solid waste disposal, for example. Many local officials have begun programs of recycling to reduce the amount of waste going into landfills. Most of these recycling programs depend on people sorting their own trash so that recyclable materials can be collected separately from waste for the landfill. If people do sort their trash, the program can succeed. If they do not, the program will not work, and officials will have to find other ways to get rid of the trash people produce.

Behavior that harms people helps shape public policy because it creates a problem that local government attempts to reduce through regulation. When some people in a community indicate that they are offended, annoyed, or hurt by others' actions, local officials have to respond. The officials may decide that the action is so harmful that it should be regulated, or they may decide that the action is not causing enough of a problem to justify regulation.

Influencing Public Policy

Talking directly to public officials is one very important way to influence policy. People call officials or visit them in person to discuss problems they think require government attention. Or they may speak at public hearings or other meetings attended by public officials. Letters to public officials or petitions signed by large numbers of people are also ways people communicate their views about what government should do.

Often it is important to organize public support for a proposal. Officials are frequently persuaded by the reasons people provide in arguing for or against a proposal, but they can also be persuaded

Franklin County residents hold up signs expressing their opposition to the site commissioners have chosen for a new jail while their spokesperson addresses the commissioners during a board meeting.

by seeing that large numbers of people agree. To organize support, people publicize the problem and the response they think government should make. They may hold news conferences or demonstrations to get the attention of newspapers, radio, and television. They may also write letters to the editor. Speaking to clubs and other organizations about the problem and proposed solutions is another way to gain support. So are holding meetings about the problem, mailing information to people likely to be interested, and encouraging people to discuss the issue with their friends and neighbors.

People can and do seek to use government for their own personal purposes, of course. But many people are also interested in helping make the entire community a better place to live and work. People may disagree about whether a particular proposal is in the public interest, and debate is important. Asking how the community is improved by a proposal helps focus attention on the public benefits of government action. People who want the government to act should be able to explain how they think the proposed action will help improve conditions generally.

Good government depends on the public being aware of the problems and opportunities facing the community. Good government requires that many people learn about public issues and try to influence public policy. Good government requires that people register and vote. Good government requires that many people volunteer to help government, including running for elective office. Good government requires that many well qualified people make full-time careers serving as employees of local government. Good government will increasingly depend on you, as you become an adult in your community.

For Further Reading

BOOKS

The Big Click: Photographs of One Day in North Carolina April 21, 1989, Mobility, Inc. Richmond, VA, 1989.
This collection of color photos taken by numerous photographers shows different activities that people in North Carolina undertake at similar times in a single day.

Bledsoe, Jerry, *Carolina Curiosities - Jerry Bledsoe's outlandish guide to the dadblamedest things to see and do in North Carolina*, Fast and McMillan Publishers, Inc., Charlotte, NC, 1984.
This funny guidebook of places to see and things to do in North Carolina includes the site of Babe Ruth's first home run, Hog Day, the home of the man with the world's strongest teeth and other oddities.

Coates, Albert, *The People and their Government*, self published, 1977.
A discussion of citizen participation in local government identifies volunteer positions in local governments.

Corbitt, David Leroy, *The Formation of the North Carolina Counties 1663-1943*, State Department of Archives, Raleigh, NC, 1969.
This history of North Carolina counties includes how they evolved and changes to their geographical boundaries.

Couch, Ernie and Jill Couch, *North Carolina Trivia*, Rutledge Hill Press, Nashville, TN, 1986.
This fun trivia book about North Carolina includes questions on geography, history, sports and science.

Crutchfield, James, *The North Carolina Almanac and Book of Facts*, Rutledge Hill Press, Nashville, TN, 1988.
This extensive collection of all kind of facts about North Carolina discusses prominent North Carolinians and the history of the state.

Bell, A. Fleming II, ed., *County Government in North Carolina*, 3rd. ed. Institute of Government, University of North Carolina at Chapel Hill, Chapel Hill, NC, 1989.
Written for county officials to use as a reference, this book includes information about administering county government, elections, property taxes and social services.

Gade, Ole and H. Daniel Stillwell, *North Carolina: People and Environment*, Geo-APP, Boone, NC, 1986.
This compilation of geographical information and other data about cities, counties, and rural areas in North Carolina includes predictions about the future of each region.

Grey, Gibson, ed. *Community Problems and Opportunities in North Carolina*, (self-published), Lumberton, NC, 1989.
This book discusses possible solutions to problems faced by local governments in North Carolina.

Jones, H.G., *North Carolina Illustrated 1524-1984*, University of North Carolina Press, Chapel Hill, NC, 1983.
This book is an extensive collection of historical photos from North Carolina with explanations of the significance of each photo.

Lawrence, David and Warren J. Wicker, ed., *Municipal Government in North Carolina*, Institute of Government, University of North Carolina at Chapel Hill, Chapel Hill, NC, 1982.
Written as a reference for city officials, this book includes the history, roles and forms of municipal government in North Carolina and sections on environmental affairs, community development, budgeting and law enforcement.

Luebke, Paul, *Tarheel Politics: Myths and Realities*, University of North Carolina Press, Chapel Hill, NC, 1990.
This discussion of politics in North Carolina describes conflicts between the "modernizers," who want to transform the state, and the "traditionalists," who feel change is unnecessary.

Massengill, Steven and Robert Topkins, *A North Carolina Postcard Album 1905-1925*, Division of Archives and History, North Carolina Department of Cultural Resources, Raleigh, NC, 1988.
This collection of picture postcards depicts North Carolina people and scenes in the early years of this century.

Powell, William S., *Dictionary of North Carolina Biography*, University of North Carolina Press, Chapel Hill, NC, 1979.
This four volume set of biographies includes prominent North Carolina citizens who have made a difference in the state.

————*North Carolina: A Bicentennial History*, Norton, New York, NY, 1977.
This history of North Carolina from the colonial period to the 1970s gives readers a thorough background of the state.

————*The North Carolina Gazetteer*, University of North Carolina Press, Chapel Hill, NC, 1968.
This geographical dictionary of North Carolina discusses how land formations, lakes, mountains, rivers, towns, and counties in the state got their names.

Schumann, Marguerite, *The Living Land: An Outdoor Guide to North Carolina*, Dale Press of Chapel Hill, Chapel Hill, NC, 1977.
This guide to natural areas in North Carolina includes listings of lakes, forests, mountains, and beaches that are accessible to the public.

PERIODICALS

County Lines, Raleigh, NC: North Carolina Association of County Commissioners.
This newsletter discusses information and issues about counties in North Carolina and the people who work for those counties.

NC Insight, Raleigh, NC: North Carolina Center for Public Policy Research.
Written by the North Carolina Center for Public Policy Research, this journal presents North Carolina policy issues and makes recommendations for improving public policies.

North Carolina Historical Review, Raleigh, NC: North Carolina Historical Commission.
This compilation of articles about the history of North Carolina includes important people, events and anecdotes.

Popular Government, Chapel Hill, NC: University of North Carolina Institute of Government.
This journal contains articles about North Carolina government and current concerns of its citizens.

Southern Cities, Raleigh, NC: North Carolina League of Municipalities.
This newsletter includes stories about the people in city and town government, issues facing municipal government, and innovative programs for dealing with these problems.

Sponsors

Municipalities

Ahoskie	Brookford	Dover	Harrels
Alamance	Bryson City	Drexel	Harrellsville
Albemarle	Burgaw	Dunn	Havelock
Apex	Burlington	Durham	Henderson
Alexander Mills	Cameron	East Spencer	Hendersonville
Alliance	Canton	Edenton	Hertford
Andrews	Carolina Beach	Elkin	Hickory
Angier	Carthage	Ellenboro	High Point
Archdale	Cary	Ellerbe	Hildebran
Arlington	Catawba	Elm City	Hillsborough
Asheville	Chadbourn	Elon College	Hobgood
Atlantic Beach	Chapel Hill	Emerald Isle	Hoffman
Aurora	Charlotte	Enfield	Holden Beach
Ayden	Cherryville	Erwin	Holly Ridge
Badin	China Grove	Fairmont	Holly Springs
Bald Head Island	Chocowinity	Faith	Hookerton
Banner Elk	Claremont	Falcon	Hope Mills
Battleboro	Clayton	Farmville	Hot Springs
Bayboro	Clemmons	Fayetteville	Huntersville
Bear Grass	Clinton	Fletcher	Jackson
Beaufort	Coats	Forest City	Jacksonville
Beech Mountain	Cofield	Franklin	Jamestown
Belhaven	Como	Franklinton	Kelford
Belmont	Concord	Fuquay-Varina	Kenansville
Belville	Connelly Springs	Garland	Kenly
Benson	Conover	Garner	Kernersville
Bethel	Conway	Gibson	Kill Devil Hills
Beulaville	Cooleemee	Gibsonville	King
Biscoe	Cornelius	Glen Alpine	Kings Mountain
Bessemer City	Cove City	Goldsboro	Kinston
Biltmore Forest	Creedmoor	Graham	Kitty Hawk
Black Creek	Dallas	Granite Falls	Knightdale
Black Mountain	Danbury	Granite Quarry	Kure Beach
Boiling Spring Lakes	Davidson	Greensboro	Lake Waccamaw
Boone	Dillsboro	Greenville	Landis
Brevard	Dobbins Heights	Grimesland	Laurel Park
Broadway	Dortches	Hamlet	Laurinburg

Lawndale
Leland
Lenoir
Lewisvili.E
Lexington
Liberty
Lincolnton
Linden
Long Beach
Long View
Lumber Bridge
Lumberton
Macclesfield
Madison
Maggie Valley
Maiden
Manteo
Marion
Mars Hill
Marshall
Marshville
Matthews
Maxton
Mayodan
Mcadenville
Mcdonald
Mcfarlan
Mesic
Middlesex
Milton
Minnesott Beach
Mocksville
Monroe
Montreat
Mooresville
Morganton
Morrisville
Mount Airy
Mount Gilead

Mount Olive
Murfreesboro
Murphy
Nags Head
Nashville
New Bern
New London
Newport
Newton
Newton Grove
Norlina
North Topsail Beach
North Wilkesboro
Ocean Isle Beach
Old Fort
Oxford
Pilot Mountain
Pine Knoll Shores
Pine Level
Pinehurst
Pinetops
Pittsboro
Plymouth
Pollocksville
Princeton
Raeford
Ramseur
Raleigh
Red Oak
Reidsville
Richfield
Richlands
Roanoke Rapids
Robersonville
Robbins
Rocky Mount
Rolesville
Roseboro
Rural Hall

Rutherford College
Rutherfordton
Salemburg
Salisbury
Sanford
Scotland Neck
Selma
Seven Devils
Seven Springs
Shelby
Siler City
Simpson
Smithfield
Snow Hill
Southern Pines
Southern Shores
Spindale
Spring Lake
Spruce Pine
Stallings
Stanfield
Stanley
Stantonsburg
Star
Statesville
Stedman
St. Helena
St. Pauls
Stoneville
Sugar Mountain
Sunset Beach
Surf City
Swansboro
Sylva
Tarboro
Taylorsville
Taylortown
Thomasville
Topsail Beach

Trent Woods
Troutman
Troy
Tryon
Valdese
Vandemere
Varnamtown
Vass
Wade
Wadesboro
Wake Forest
Wallace
Walnut Creek
Walstonburg
Washington
Waynesville
Weaverville
Webster
Weddington
Wendell
West Jefferson
Whispering Pines
Whitakers
Whiteville
White Lake
Whitsett
Williamston
Wilmington
Wilson
Windsor
Wingate
Winston-Salem
Winton
Woodfin
Wrightsville Beach
Yadkinville
Yanceyville
Yaupon Beach
Zebulon

Counties

Alamance	Dare	Macon	Rutherford
Alexander	Duplin	Madison	Sampson
Alleghany	Durham	Martin	Scotland
Beaufort	Edgecombe	Mcdowell	Stanly
Bertie	Forsyth	Mecklenburg	Stokes
Buncombe	Franklin	Mitchell	Surry
Burke	Gaston	Montgomery	Swain
Cabarrus	Gates	Moore	Transylvania
Caldwell	Graham	Nash	Tyrrell
Camden	Granville	New Hanover	Union
Carteret	Greene	Northampton	Vance
Caswell	Halifax	Onslow	Wake
Catawba	Harnett	Orange	Warren
Chatham	Haywood	Pamlico	Washington
Cherokee	Henderson	Pasquotank	Watauga
Chowan	Hertford	Person	Wayne
Clay	Hoke	Perquimans	Wilkes
Cleveland	Hyde	Pitt	Wilson
Columbus	Iredell	Polk	Yadkin
Craven	Johnston	Randolph	Yancey
Cumberland	Jones	Richmond	
Currituck	Lee	Robeson	
Davie	Lenoir	Rockingham	

The following organizations have contributed to this book:

North Carolina Association of County Commissioners
North Carolina City and County Management Association
North Carolina League of Municipalities

Glossary/Index

Absentee ballot, an official list of candidates on which voters who cannot get to the polling place on election day indicate their votes, 124

"Adopt a Highway" program, 66

Aid to Families with Dependent Children (AFDC), financial aid to families that do not have enough money for basic needs, like housing and food. AFDC is a federal program but is administered by county departments of social services in North Carolina, 37, 109

Alcoholic Beverage Control (ABC), 34–35, 37, 121

Aldermen, 21, 116, 120

Allocate, to set aside money for a specific purpose, 35, 38

Annexation, the legal process of extending municipal boundaries and adding territory to a city or town, 20

Appropriate, to authorize the amounts of money government can spend, 100, 117

Assessed value, the value assigned to property by government to establish its worth for tax purposes, 102–104

Assessment, a charge imposed on property owners for building streets, sidewalks, water lines, sewers, or other improvements government makes to the property, 109

Ballot, an official list of candidates on which the voter indicates his or her votes, 82, 120, 124

Board of Education, State, 35, 40

Board of Health, State, 16

Bond, a loan to governments that is made when people buy the government's commitment to repay the loan, plus interest, 5, 101–102, 106

Budget, 21, 35, 37, 40–41, 96–97, 99–101, 104, 109, 117

Business development corporation, a group of people legally organized as a corporation to encourage economic development, 70–71

Capital, facilities used to produce services. Local governments' capital includes land, buildings, equipment, water and sewer lines, city streets and bridges, 100–102

Chairman, 117

Chamber of commerce, a group of business people formed to promote business interests in the community, 68

Charter, the document defining how a city or town is to be governed and giving it legal authority to act as a local government, 19–20, 82

Citation, an official summons to appear before a court to answer a charge of violating a government regulation, 93

Civil, concerning government's role in relations among citizens. Civil violations are different than criminal violations in that they are not offenses against all the people and are not prosecuted by the district attorney. When governments are involved in civil disputes, they are simply another party in the case, just like a person or a private corporation. 93

Clerk of Court, 34

Coastal plain, the eastern region of North Carolina, extending approximately 150 miles inland from the coast. The western border of the region is usually defined as the western boundaries of Northhampton, Halifax, Nash, Johnston, Harnett, Hoke, and Scotland counties. This region includes 41 counties. 30, 32

Community-focused services, 65

Community Development Block Grants, 109

Compost, decayed material which is used as fertilizer, 42, 51, 54

Constitution, North Carolina, 34, 80, 102, 117

Constitution, United States, 5, 80, 123

Contract, an agreement made between two or more people or organizations, 18, 26, 53, 66, 102, 116

Coroner, 34

Corporation, a group of persons formed by law to act as a single body, 18–19, 26, 115

Council, 7, 12, 20–21, 24, 75–76, 82, 88, 91, 98–100. 102, 105, 116, 120, 122

Council member, 21, 99, 116, 120

Council-manager plan, an arrangement for local government in which the elected legislature hires a professional executive to direct government activities, 21

County Commissioners, 12, 34–42, 76, 85, 103, 105, 110, 116

Crime, an act that is forbidden by law. A crime is an offense against all of the people of the state, not just the victim of the act, 2, 37, 46, 58–63, 75, 80, 117

Debt service, payments of principal and interest on a loan, 100

Department of Transportation, State, 42, 66

Desalination, the process by which the salt is taken out of sea water, 47

Developer, a person or business that builds houses or prepares land for building, 71, 90

Dispatcher, a person who gives emergency workers information so that those workers can respond to emergencies, 58

Economic development, activities to create new jobs and additional sales and other business, 65, 68, 72, 76, 84, 103

Education, 34–36, 40, 100, 115

Elections, 20, 34–37, 110–121, 124

Employees, 9, 21–24, 33, 40, 45, 68, 78, 97–99, 104, 109, 113–117

Enteric, 16

Expenditures, money spent, 35, 96–100

Extraterritorial land-use planning jurisdiction, the area outside city limits over which a city has authority for planning and regulating land use, 85

Favoritism, hiring or giving favorable treatment to an employee because of friendship, 114

Federal, a system with separate state and national governments. The United States has a federal system of government. We also use the term "federal government" to refer to the national government of the United States. 5–7, 35, 37–38, 47, 53–56, 103, 109, 126, 123

Fiscal year, (FY) the twelve-month period used by government for record keeping, budgeting, taxing, and other aspects of financial management, 97–98, 100, 104, 110

Food Stamps, a program to help people with financial need buy food. The program issues vouchers to be used like money for purchasing food. This is a federal program, but is administered by county departments of social services in North Carolina, 6, 37, 109

Fund balance, money a government has not spent at the end of its fiscal year, 96–97, 99, 103–105, 109

Gasoline tax, a tax placed on purchases of gasoline, 106

General Assembly, North Carolina, 15–16, 18–20, 25, 28, 34, 42, 80, 92, 99, 105

General obligation bond, a loan that a government agrees to repay using tax money, even if the tax rate must be raised, 101

Grant, money given by state or federal government to local governments to fund local projects, 5, 6, 70, 109

Green box sites, 52–53

Greensboro Against Smoking Pollution (GASP), 82–84

Greenspace, an area that is kept undeveloped to provide more open land in or near a city, 90

Ground water, water that collects underground, 46–47, 54

Highway Patrol, State, 62

Hugo, Hurricane, 3

Human Relations Commissions, 72-75

Impurities, materials that pollute or keep whatever they are in from being pure, 47

Incident report, a report that a police officer writes describing a crime or other problem situation, 58

Incineration, the safe burning of wastes, 54

Incorporation, the legal process of creating a new corporation, 19

Independent Boards, 35, 42

Infrastructure, basic public services such as water, sewers, and roads that are needed for economic development, 68

Initiative, a way in which citizens propose laws by gathering voter signatures on a petition. Only a few cities and no counties in North Carolina are authorized to use initiative. 82, 84

Installment-purchase agreement, an arrangement to buy something in which the buyer gets to use the item while paying for it in regularly scheduled payments. If the buyer fails to complete payments, the seller can reclaim the property, 102

Institute of Government, 96

Interest, a charge for borrowed money that the borrower agrees to pay the lender, 67, 71, 100, 102, 109

Interest rate, a percentage of the amount borrowed that the borrower agrees to pay to the lender as a charge for the use of the lender's money, 102

Property tax, a tax placed on the assessed value of property to be paid by the owner of that property, 96, 102–105, 107, 109–110

Property tax rate, a percentage of the assessed value of property that determines how much tax is due for that property. In North Carolina property tax rates are expressed as dollars of tax per hundred dollars of assessed value. Thus, a tax rate of $.50 means that each property owner must pay $.50 for each $100 of property he or she owns. 103–104, 109

Proponent, a person or organization that supports a proposal, 77

Proposal, a suggestion put forward for approval, 76–78, 93, 99, 117, 119

Public health, 15, 33, 37, 39–40, 80

Public hearings, 24, 93, 119, 126

Real property, land and buildings and other improvements on it, 102

References, people who know how well someone did on a previous job or about that person's other qualifications for a job, 115

Referendum, an election in which citizens vote directly on a public policy question, 9, 82–84, 93, 102

Regional council, an organization of local governments to deal with their mutual problems. There are 18 regional councils covering North Carolina. 7

Register of Deeds, 27, 34–37, 90, 117, 122

Revenue, the amount of money that a government receives, 96–111

Revenue bond, a loan that a government agrees to pay off from fees collected though operating the facility built with that loan, 102

Rural, area where not many people live. The area outside cities and towns. 25, 30–33, 42, 46, 62, 66, 91

Sales tax, a tax on each purchase paid by the buyer at the time of purchase, 104–105

School board, 12, 34, 40–41, 117, 121

Sedimentation, 47

Septic tank, a container in which wastes are broken down by bacteria, 49

Sheriff, 26–27, 34–35, 37, 43, 57–59, 117, 120, 122

Sludge, the solid material separated from sewage, 49

Social services, 34–37, 75, 115, 121

Special-use permits, 88

Stereotype, a set of untested beliefs about the members of a group, 68

Subdivision regulation, rules for dividing land for development, 85, 90–91

Subsidize, to reduce the amount users pay for a service by funding some of the cost from another source, 107

Subsidy, a payment which reduces the cost to the user, 107

Sue, to ask a court to act against a person or organization to prevent or pay for damage by that person or organization, 18

Suffrage, 123

Surface water, water in lakes or streams, 46

Tax base, the value of the property, sales, or income being taxed, 103, 106

Thoroughfares, 91

Total assessed value, the sum of the assessed value of all the property a city or county can tax, 103

Unincorporated, the part of a county outside the cities and towns in that county, 26, 33, 42, 50, 52, 57, 85, 92, 116

Urban, area where people live close together. Most urban areas in North Carolina have been incorporated as municipalities. 18, 20, 25, 30

User-focused services, 46, 63, 65

User fees, 102, 106–111, 117

Vandalism, 57

Variance, permission to do something that is different from what is allowed by current regulations, 88

Volunteers, people who donate their time and effort, 24, 68, 113, 115–116, 122

Voting, 9, 73, 82, 122–124

Ward, a section of a jurisdiction for voting, representative, or administrative purposes, 119

Watershed, an area that drains water into a stream or lake, 46

Zoning, rules designating different areas of land for different uses. For instance, some land might be zoned for houses, other land for stores, and still other land for factories. 85–90, 93

Glossary/Index